This book is dedicated to all of the quitters who have made Key West their home.

ACKNOWLEDGEMENTS

It would be impossible to thank everybody who helped make this book possible. While it would be expected that we thank our families and friends for their support and assistance, the fact of the matter is that this book would not have been written were it not for the jackasses in the big cities that made us think twice about the quality of life we were living.

To all of the incompetent middle managers who berated their employees; to the guy who cut us off in traffic and then gave us the finger; to the automated customer service menus that went out of their way to prevent human contact; to the corporate giants who wanted a robot working for them rather than a human being, thank you.

Our lives are much better because of you.

CONTENTS

PART 1
Changes in Latitudes
(This could be the place for you.)

Quit Your Job
And Move To
Key West
The Complete Guide

Christopher Shultz   David L. Sloan

PHANTOM PRESS
KEY WEST, FLORIDA

Slammin' cover design: Kerry Karshna
Stunning cover photo: RobOneal.com
Congratulations! You have a collector's edition.

10 9 8 7 6 5 4 3 2 1
ISBN 9780967449814

"I've a notion to move the capital to Key West and just stay."
- President Harry S. Truman

THE CONCH REPUBLIC

90 Miles to
CUBA

SOUTHERNMOST

POINT

CONTINENTAL
U.S.A.

KEY WEST, FL
Home of the Sun Set

RobOneal.com

Quit Your Job And Move To Key West

The Complete Guide

Christopher Shultz   David L. Sloan

END OF THE RAINBOW
AND END OF THE ROUTE
KEY WEST   FLORIDA
Unlimited US 1 Opportunities
TROPICAL VACATIONLAND

Monroe County Sheriff's Department

CONTENTS

PART 2
Changes in Attitudes
(Your complete guide to becoming a local.)

Paradise City

A story from Hell

Key West. A place that immediately brings to mind images of beaches, drinking, rumrunners, writers and a lifestyle like no place else in the United States. It is an island of enchantment and mystery that attracts people from all over the world.

If you have ever visited our island, you probably have a pretty good idea why Key West is so desirable: sunshine all year long, great bars, funky shops, easy people and a party happening somewhere 24 hours a day. Add to that the fact that we are surrounded by warm waters with a living coral reef and your own hometown might not seem so exciting right now.

A guy – we'll call him Jeffery – died in a car accident with his friends and went to heaven. Upon arriving he began to explore and found it to be a pretty nice place. White, fluffy clouds all about, angels playing their harps, Jesus doing magic tricks and Moses separating oceans.

He ran into some distant relatives and family members – even his childhood dog – but after awhile Jeffery began to grow bored and decided to have a word with God.

"Hey God?" Jeffery began. "It's really nice up here and it's been great seeing some familiar faces but I really miss the friends I died with and can't seem to find them anywhere."

God pulled out a large book, turned a few pages and spoke. "It seems all of your friends are in hell. You are the only one who made it to heaven."

This did not make Jeffery happy. He scratched his head, thought for a second and after weighing his options, asked God if he could go to hell for a visit. Though it was a strange request, God issued him a weekend pass. "Go on, son, have a good time." Jeffery smiled as he packed his bags.

Unsure what to expect in hell, Jeffery was amazed at what he saw: sandy beaches, free booze, loose women. His friends were so happy to see him they dropped what they were doing and took him on a bender through hell drinking, boating, gambling and chasing the ladies. Jeffery had the time of his life – um, afterlife, that is.

3

Arriving back in heaven bleary-eyed and worn out, Jeffery walked along the fluffy clouds watching the other heavenites go about their daily activities.

"How boring," he thought. "They have so much more fun in hell." Again he decided to talk to God.

"Hey, God." Jeffery called.

"Yes? Oh, hello Jeffery. Did you have a good time in hell with your friends?"

Jeffery nodded his head. "It was amazing. I had so much fun and it is such a cool place, I think I want to move there."

God assured him this could be arranged but warned that once he had left heaven, he would be unable to return.

Jeffery thought for a moment and replied, "No offense, but I don't really want to come back here. Everything here is boring. I want excitement and I want to be with my friends."

God snapped his fingers and with a "poof" Jeffery was gone.

"Ouch!" he yelled. "What's going on?" He opened his eyes to see fire and brimstone. Satan stood above him poking him with a pitchfork and his friends stood chained beside him carrying lumps of flaming hot coals. Jeffery looked at the devil in desperation asking, "What happened? It was so much fun here when I came to visit."

Satan looked at him and laughed. "You were on vacation then, you silly mortal. Living here is a completely different story."

Living in Key West is not hell by any means, but it is not a vacation either. Just like in your current home, there are bills to pay and jobs to be done. Many people who move here don't figure out our small town until it is too late.

By using this guide you will get a much better idea of what life is like on our side of the fence. From politics and cost of living to local customs and history we try to cover it all. After reading this guide, you may decide that island life is not your cup of tea, but then again, you may just decide to quit your job and move to Key West.

Some Call It Paradise

What makes this place so special anyway?

*C*heck out any advertisement for Key West and chances are you will come across the word "paradise." "Welcome to our tropical island paradise... ." "Paradise Found." "Come stay with us on your next trip to paradise." The list goes on.

A quick check in our white pages under "P" will show you no less than 25 listings for "paradise" ranging from Paradise Attractions to Paradise Vision with beauties in between like Paradise Plumbing and Paradise Tattoo. Key West may well be the only town in the world where you can stay at the Paradise Inn, eat at the Paradise Café and read a newspaper called...you guessed it, Paradise. What makes this place so special anyway?

In this chapter we will take a look at some of the elements that make Key West such a desirable and unique location. We will also include an overview of the types of people our paradise attracts, but let's first define paradise.

The American Heritage Dictionary defines paradise as "a place or condition of perfect happiness or beauty." It goes on further to explain that it is often capitalized, indicating Paradise is a specific location. Though it would be a stretch to say that the happiness or beauty of Key West is perfect, the fact of the matter is the island has some pretty impressive qualities. A few of the most attractive are listed below.

Weather: They don't call Florida the Sunshine State for nothing. How does an average monthly rainfall of 2.89 inches sound? That's less than 35 inches a year with the majority of it (20.82 inches) falling during what we call our rainy season, from June to October. Rainstorms usually last less than an hour and the sun often shines in spite of the rain, creating some magnificent rainbows. Spend enough time in the Keys

REASON TO QUIT — **#62**

My boss is a mental midget who treats me like swill.

and you will probably see it raining on one side of the street while the other remains dry. If you don't think that's pretty cool, don't bother coming.

Temperature: This year's forecast: average high of 83.7 degrees with an average low of 71.25 degrees. Yes, we are talking Fahrenheit. Though the humidity runs high in the summer months, the plus side of this is you don't have to iron your clothes. There may be a week or two each year when a cold front passes through, but for the most part there is no need for winter clothes and most of the houses are not even equipped with heaters.

Water: Water is an important part of any island's attraction, and Key West is no different. Though our water may not be as clear and blue as some brochures depict, Key West was blessed with the only living coral reef in the continental United States and the third longest barrier reef in the world, which makes for excellent diving, snorkeling and fishing. While one body of water would be nice, Key West is surrounded by the Gulf of Mexico and the Atlantic Ocean. The water is always warm and the lack of waves makes conditions ideal for jet skis and boating.

Flora: One of the great joys of living in Key West is walking down a side street after years of living in town and discovering a plant you have never seen before. Flowers of every color bloom year round and sweet smells fill the air. Mango, banana, coconut and avocado trees are common, as are banyan, poinciana, and gumbo limbo. We may not have changing seasons, but these tropical delights are not a bad trade off.

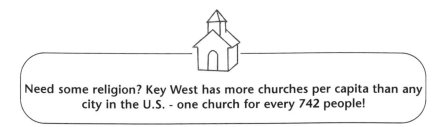

Need some religion? Key West has more churches per capita than any city in the U.S. - one church for every 742 people!

Animals: Animals are everywhere. We knew Key West was a place to call home the first time we went to the Schooner Wharf Bar and found a dog sitting on the stool next to us lapping beer out of a bowl. Though the health department keeps threatening to crack down on them, dogs are still welcome in many of our bars and restaurants. Cats are pretty common as well, the most famous having six or more toes on each paw. In fact, some houses or apartments come with a cat. When one tenant leaves, the next one just takes over feeding duties. We've had three so far that we'll still go to visit. Don't worry about allergies, they are all outdoor cats.

Chickens are everywhere. Some people love them and some hate them. Either way, it is hard not to smile when you see a mama chicken and her six babies waddling across the gas station parking lot.

Other animals you will grow to love (or at least accept) include rats, geckos, spiders, ants, palmetto bugs (that's a roach with wings,) scorpions, and of course mosquitoes. Be sure to thank the chicken for the bugs he has eaten as he crows under your window at three in the morning.

History: So history was not your favorite class in school? Don't worry. Key West has one of the most unique histories in Florida and it is chock full of bizarre facts and humorous anecdotes. Do yourself a favor and take a break from the barstool to visit the Monroe County Public Library. The Florida History Room has some incredible books on the island as well as historic maps, photos and directories.

Architecture: Next time you see the old house down the street from you being torn down to make room for a Wal-Mart parking lot, consider

REASON TO QUIT — #7

My cubical is too small and besides, it's a cubicle.

that Old Town Key West has about 3,000 structures, many of which date to the late 1800s and are listed on the National Register of Historic Places. Most early houses were built by ships' carpenters who built them from the wood of ships that had wrecked on the reef. Some houses were even built in the Bahamas, taken apart and shipped to Key West. Bad news for Wal-Mart: the houses are protected so we can all enjoy them for years to come.

Attitude: Big-city life can cause big-city strife. Key West, for many, offers a place a little more laid back, a little more accepting, a little more tolerant and a little less judgmental. Something has to be said for a place where you can dress how you want, say what you want, do what you want and be who you want without the worry of others wanting you to be something you don't want to be. We do have laws, and the police selectively enforce them. We also have our share of jackasses who can only find joy in the misery of others, but as a whole the island runs a little bit slower and a little bit softer. Jimmy Buffett said it best: "Changes in latitudes, changes in attitudes."

Legend: Legends are what any drinking town worth its weight in salt is all about. Only in Key West can you follow in the footsteps of Ernest Hemingway, tell tales of pirates and shipwrecks, explore Civil War forts, search for treasure and sunken galleons, talk of rumrunners, drug runners, prohibition, poets, writers, actors, ghosts and voodoo, all without leaving your barstool. Many stories have been passed down from islanders through the generations, while new ones are being born every day. No one in Key West is really sure how accurate these stories are, but we all agree that sharing local lore in a bar beats the hell out of flipping through 112 channels of crap on television. The legend lives on.

REASON TO QUIT —— #23

I have to wear a tie to work everyday, but I prefer Hawaiian shirts.

People: Please try to be original when asked why you came to Key West – don't say the weather or the people. Four out of five dentists recommend shooting yourself in the head for lack of originality if that is your answer. Most people are friendly (some overly so,) outgoing, accommodating, intelligent and insane. The great part is that insane people are pretty good at disguising their insanity at first, so in short doses it can be misinterpreted as good-natured fun. Don't worry. Most of the insane people here are harmless to others.

Feel free to add to the list. It's your book and you can do what you want with it, but let's continue along. Now that you know some of the reasons people are drawn to Key West, let's take a look at the types of people who live here. Keep in mind, this is a two-by-four mile island and the people we are about to describe will be your neighbors, co-workers and friends. We'll let the statistics do the talking first and then follow up with a breakdown of the cliques.

STATS

POPULATION

Year	Monroe County	Key West
1980	63,188	24,292
1990	78,024	24,832
2000	79,589	25,478
2003	80,537	25,811

2,740 Military employment in Key West in 2003

(stats continued on next page)

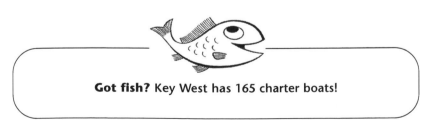

Got fish? Key West has 165 charter boats!

AGE BREAKDOWN, 2000:

Age	Monroe County	Key West
0-19	19%	18%
20-34	18%	25%
35-44	18%	19%
45-54	18%	17%
55-64	12%	10%
65-74	9%	6%
75+	6%	5%
Median Age	42.6	38.9

POPULATION BY RACE, 2000:

	Monroe County	Key West
White	77.2%	71.4%
Black	4.5%	8.8%
Hispanic	15.8%	16.5%
Other	2.5%	3.3%

Conchs: These are people who were born in Key West. If you were not born in Key West, you are not, have not been, and never will be a Conch. Don't try to be – it won't happen. Some people feel an underlying tension between Conchs and non- Conchs, but the fact remains, these are the people who helped make the island what it is today. Show respect, my bubba!

The Gay Community: An estimated 20 to 25 percent of our population is gay. If you come from Mars, now would be a good time for us to point out that gay means more than happy. The island's live-and-let-live

Drink much? Key West consumes more alcohol per capita than any city in the U.S.

attitude has created a haven for gays and strives to set an example for other communities. If you have problems accepting the sexual preferences of others, keep your mouth shut or don't bother coming. Check out the Key West Business Guild and the Gay and Lesbian Community Center for updated information on gay events.

The Military: Key West has held important military significance since before the Civil War. Though the actual number of personnel stationed in Key West is classified information, our Armed Forces here are dominated by the Navy and Coast Guard.

The Cuban Community: In the 2000 census, 16.5 percent of our residents were Hispanic, most of them of Cuban heritage with a Key West history that dates back to our earliest roots. Ninety miles from Cuba would you expect anything less? A few cultural delights that can still be enjoyed in Key West include hand-rolled cigars, Cuban-mix sandwiches, and a variety of coffee drinks that will grow hair on your chest and erase Starbuck's from your evil latte mind. Though cockfighting has been outlawed, Cuban folk art, Latin dancing, salsa music, and the world-famous mojito rum drink can all still be found. Key West is also home to the Cuban-American Heritage Festival.

The Black Community: In the 2000 census 8.8 percent of our population is listed as black or African-American. Most of the African-American community lives in Bahama Village, an area west of Whitehead Street and south of Angela Street. Many locals would agree this is the last little piece of a real community in Key West. Kids play

Relatives coming? Key West has 573 hotels, guesthouses and rentals that make up 5,300 units.

in the street, people know their neighbors, chickens wander around crowing at all hours of the day and night, and a seat on the porch is preferred to a seat in front of the TV.

The Art Community: Key West has a strong draw for artists of all types. Actors, writers, singers, painters, poets, songwriters, sculptors and others all call Key West home. Some are famous, some not yet. Many do it for money while others do it for joy. The end result is self-expression, art and cultural events around every corner.

Retirees: Twenty-one percent of our population is past the retirement age. Work hard, save your money and you, too, could join this intelligent group of people. Most of our retired residents only live here for the winter months. The summer is spent up north until the cold weather comes and the southern migration begins again. Some locals use the term snowbird like it is a bad thing. In reality, we're jealous.

Families: Believe it or not, there are people who raise families in Key West. Like the mystical Incan tribes, we don't know who they are or what they do, but they exist.

Street People: If you're going to be homeless, why not do it where it's warm? Key West has a homeless problem. We also have a hippie circuit that begs on the street, panhandlers, beggars and more. Before you support their cause, realize that some, if not all of these people are banking over $100 dollars a day.

REASON TO QUIT ── **#3**

I spend more time in traffic than I do at home.

The Hospitality Community: Sixty-three percent of our residents are employed by the hospitality industry making this the largest group with a common bond by far. It includes bar and restaurant workers, hotel employees, cab drivers, travel agents, tour guides and more. Some people have been here for years while others are just passing through. Some are young, some are old. These are the people who shape the true image of Key West for all of the tourists that come to town.

Escape Artists: As you spend time in Key West you will begin to see that everybody here is escaping from something. For some people it's the law, for others a divorce or job failure. Some people just want to get away from city life, but everybody is escaping something. Key West is the end of the line. When you get here there's no going south and staying in the United States. Scientists are working, as we speak, to locate the part of the human brain that amazes them most. It is probably the section that tells people who are running away, "Go to Key West." Isn't science amazing?

There you have it, the people of Key West condensed into one easy-to-read chapter. In summary, everyone comes here because they are running from something...well, that, the weather and the people.

Get a job! Monroe County boasts an unemployment rate of 2.1%.

Monroe County Public Library

Our First Quitters

A brief history of working life in Key West

What's in a name?

Unlike most cities, Key West has had many names, each with its own strange meaning. The first people to live and die in Key West were Native Americans. The first visitors to the island were Spaniards looking for safe trade routes through the Straits of Florida.

After a particularly nasty Indian massacre, the island was left littered with bones and soon became a sacred burial ground for the natives; they supposedly thought this to be a magical place and the best place to spend your life after death. (Hey, we wouldn't mind being buried here.)

The Spaniards, upon arrival, found bones everywhere, and accordingly named the tiny spot of land "Cayo Hueso" that literally translates to "Isle of Bones."

Something wasn't too appealing about the name "bone island," so as time went on the Spanish term was corrupted. "Cayo" became "Key" and "Hueso" became "West." The name really has nothing to do with the fact that it is the westernmost key in the island chain.

Over the years a few attempts were made to change the name to something more desirable. Thompson's Island and Allenton came close, but most of the people creating the navigational charts of the day stuck with Key West, which has remained the official name for more than a century.

Unofficially, Key West has a number of names. Locals call Key West "The Rock" because, after all, it is simply one big rock. The term "Conch Republic" came into regular use after our secession from the United States in 1982. (Don't worry, we surrendered and they took us back.) "Cayo Hueso" is still used by our Spanish population but most of us just call it home. Spend enough time and we're sure you will do the same.

Spare some change? The average panhandler in Key West makes more than $100 a day. So does the average waiter.

Our First Settlers and Their New Jobs

The first known visitor to Key West was Ponce de Leon. He discovered the island in 1513 during his search for the Fountain of Youth. It is believed neither he, nor his crew, ever came to shore due to the risk of jagged rocks and extremely difficult sailing conditions. Little did good ol' Ponce realize that Key West is probably the closest thing to the Fountain of Youth in existence.

For years, Key West was left to the pirates. The conditions it offered including water shallow enough for their sloops, but too shallow for other boats to pursue them; an abundance of mangroves in which to hide, and close proximity to the major shipping channels were ideal. After raping and pillaging they could also hide out here and take a break.

As time passed, many ships wrecked, and the Native American tribe of Calusa Indians, pretty much kept the island to themselves. Realizing what a treasure the land was, the United States government decided to come in and do its part. In the 1820s the U.S. Navy came down to fight off the pirates, and soon the first legitimate quitters arrived. Most of the Indians relocated, and those who were unfortunate enough to stay died from new diseases the quitters brought with them.

In order to make a living, early settlers of the Keys had pineapple farms and the fruit was considered a delicacy. The fishing industry started to boom and a shark-processing factory was launched in Big Pine Key. Business was good, but there was no sense of adventure. Soon, a new industry was born.

Located on a major shipping trade route with a conveniently treacherous reef, island residents were often called upon to rescue ships

Not Cheap! The average two-bedroom home in Key West costs $700,000 and will be selling for even more by the time you read this.

in distress. They thought as long as they were out there, they might as well make a living from it, and thus came the wreckers. The city thrived on salvaging goods from the wrecked ships, so much so that some of the locals deliberately lured ships onto the reef. Nobody knows what truly happened, but Key West soon became the wealthiest city per capita in the United States.

As Key West flourished, more people started moving here, bringing more money. Key Westers soon starting branching out, going into business and selling the goods that are famous today.

Cigars: Cigar makers from Cuba established factories in Key West and the industry thrived. Pretty soon everyone had to have a Cuban cigar. The business was crippled after most of the factories were destroyed in the great fire – talk about lighting up – and the manufacturers relocated to Tampa. Today the smoke has cleared, and with the resurgence of the cigar as a status symbol, the industry is thriving here once again – although not with Cuban tobacco.

Fishing: In 1949, shrimp were being harvested commercially here for the first time and people found them shrimply delicious. The money they generated quickly earned them the nickname "pink gold." Other delicacies pulled from Keys waters included yellowtail snapper, wahoo, grouper, dolphin and more. Shrimpers continue to ply their trade in our offshore waters, and there are more than 165 charter fishing boats in service.

Welcome mat! More than three million people
visit the Florida Keys every year.

Sponging: First off, we're talking sea sponges, not that tattered pink thing sitting by your kitchen sink, though they are closely related. Our warm, shallow waters create the ideal conditions for sea sponges. Key West's spongers would free-dive and collect the sponges for exportation. The industry thrived until Greek spongers – with the advantage of air tanks – picked the waters clean. The sponge was able to make a comeback and now the unlucky ones end up by your kitchen sink, while the lucky ones end up in pretty, rich people's claw-footed bathtubs.

Military: The U.S. Navy, which had driven off the pirates a century earlier, came to the rescue again by turning Key West into a submarine base. This brought government money to build bases and along with it came the submariners. Some say this was the first influx of the gay scene in Key West. Submariner bars started popping up everywhere. The joke went around town that if you send 100 men down in a sub, when they come back you have 50 couples. (Insert laugh here.)

The Coming of Tourism: In the 1930s Key West went bankrupt due to the depression, mismanagement, corrupt local government, crooks and criminals. Something had to be done, and though the U.S. government proposed moving everybody to the mainland, the officials of the island realized they had something no other place in the United States of America had: an island with great weather, sunshine, great fishing, incredible stories and the possibility of anything happening. When things were summed up, it was decided that Key West would be marketed as a tourist destination. Henry Flagler built his impossible "railroad that went to sea" and soon the wealthy tourists came to relax in the lap of luxury.

REASON TO QUIT — #52

I'd rather be fishing.

Beautiful hotels were built, bars flourished and the nightlife never ended. It was an untouched place and the wealthy came to be surrounded by the enchantment of the isle. In the years that followed, the island experienced highs and lows in the economy. In the 1980s tourism became the major industry but remained mostly seasonal. Tourism has become a year-round market as more and more people discover the treasures the island offers.

Key West Today: The island has gone through its share of changes. Instead of pirates cruising the waters we have sunset sails. Instead of the great railroad (it was destroyed by the Labor Day Hurricane of 1935), we have the Conch Tour Train. The one thing Key West has kept is its mystery and the legendary feeling that you are in Never-Never Land. You might not see a rumrunner but you can feel that they walked on your street and possibly drank in your house. This mystery and enchantment is why millions of people come here and why the lucky few of us live here.

To this day, Key West attracts people from all over the world. The island has this magical way of getting people to drop their guard, let loose and do things they would never normally do.

Oops! The southernmost point marker is not on the southernmost point.

Famous People Who Moved to Key West

Key West's live-and-let-live attitude has always been appealing to celebrities. Some famous people liked it so much they decided to stay for a while. Here are a few of the better known ones.

1. Ernest Hemingway - writer
2. Jimmy Buffett - singer/songwriter/author
3. Kelly McGillis - Actress
4. Harry Truman - President of the United States
5. Judy Blume - writer
6. Hunter S. Thompson - writer
7. Tennessee Williams - writer
8. Robert Frost - poet
9. Betty Page - sex symbol
10. Calvin Klein - designer
11. Jean Beauvoir - musician
12. Truman Capote - playwright
13. Thomas Edison - inventor
14. Hulk Hogan - wrestler
15. Roy Scheider - actor
16. Divine - actor/actress/drag queen
17. Shel Silverstein - author/artist
18. Christopher Shultz and David Sloan - famous authors

REASON TO QUIT — #81

One more memo and I'll go postal.

Time For The Test

Do you have what it takes?

Are You Ready For Key West?
TAKE THE QUIZ AND SEE HOW YOU SCORE

1. My current climate is:
a) Covered in snow nine months of the year with three days of sunshine in early July.
b) Hot and dry, heat stroke advisories are common.
c) Quite cold in the winter, but the other seasons are very nice.
d) Eighty degrees and sunny all year with low humidity and occasional rain.

2. The following best describes my feelings about African-Americans, homosexuals, Cubans and other diverse groups:
a) We're all one human family.
b) I judge people as individuals, not groups.
c) See no evil, hear no evil, speak no evil.
d) I'm not prejudiced, I hate everybody equally.

3. My choice of transportation on a 2 x 4 mile island would be:
a) My feet or bicycle.
b) A purple moped with a "born to be wild" sticker.
c) A Hummer, Suburban, or gas guzzling S.U.V.
d) My Winnebago, naturally.

4. For an apartment, I would be willing to pay:
a) $1250 a month (plus utilities, first last and security deposit) for a shoebox-sized one bedroom with termites, ants, a leaky sink and 1950s kitchen appliances.
b) $900 a month for the same apartment 16 miles out of Key West.
c) $800 a month for a small studio apartment with palmetto bugs (cockroaches with wings) the size of my sister.
d) $650 for a nice two-bedroom in a quiet part of town without any neighbors close by. A swimming pool and hot tub would be nice too.

REASON TO QUIT — #69

I've slept with everyone I work with.

5. When it comes to working, I would like:
a) Three low-paying jobs that allow me to pay most of my bills on time and still buy a drink after work.
b) Two low-paying jobs and one day off a week.
c) Two well-paying jobs and two days off a week
d) I'm gonna be a bartender, man!

6. I like to be awakened by:
a) Roosters crowing at all hours, construction crews and moped horns (Beep! Beep!)
b) Drunk drag queens bitch-slapping each other outside my window.
c) My alarm clock.
d) Songbirds chirping, children playing and a cool morning breeze.

7. My favorite extracurricular activities include:
a) Drinking, drinking and drinking.
b) Water sports and drinking.
c) Going to the mall, concerts and an occasional drink.
d) Bowling, mountain climbing and opera. I hate bars.

8. When I go out in the evening I like:
a) Pricey drinks served by surly bartenders in dirty bars with ear-splitting Jimmy Buffett covers playing through antiquated systems.
b) Pricey drinks in somewhat clean bars with acoustic Jimmy Buffett covers and friendly, but incompetent, bartenders.
c) Cheap drinks, friendly service and an occasional Jimmy Buffett song.
d) Rock-bottom prices, exceptional service and no Jimmy Buffett songs.

9. When I go to the movies I expect:
a) Sticky floors, dirty seats, poor sound, poor picture quality and plenty of disruptions. (ring, ring, hello!)
b) A decent selection of some current blockbusters and a cool art cinema with a couple of screens.
c) The movie I want to see when I want to see it.
d) Supersonic Dolby surround sound, recliner-style stadium seating, digital super screen and all of the current releases.

How Did You Score?

Mostly A: Pack your bags and come on down. Key West will welcome you with open arms.

Mostly B: Come down for a long vacation before quitting your job. Key West will have a lot to offer, but you will need to make a few adjustments.

Mostly C: Better not quit your day job. It's time you realize life is not fair and you can't have everything you want…especially in Key West.

Mostly D: Read no further. Put the book down and go back to reality. Key West will chew you up and spit you out.

The good old days. Key West used to have a
bowling alley, roller rink, miniature golf course, dog track
and a drive-in movie theater.

Quit Your Job

Go on. You can do it.

One of the first things you should consider when preparing to leave your job and come to Key West is this: most folks who move here don't stay long.

People often speak of the mystery our island possesses, but everyone is at a loss to explain it. The same mystery exists in the island's human-like ability to choose who will stay and who must go. While the television show *Survivor* has been a hit for several years, Key West has been voting people off the island since the first Native Americans visited several thousand years ago. (Instead of fame and lucrative product endorsements they received the consolation prize of death.)

Some people get too wrapped up in the party scene. Others have trouble making new friends. Good jobs can be hard to find and expenses can be steep. Some people hate it here but can't leave while others love it and can't stay. The list goes on and on, but the fact of the matter is that even though you choose Key West, Key West may not accept you.

Most people spend between one and three years on the island before packing their bags. Key West is an ideal place for someone to take a year or two off relaxing in the sunshine and strangeness. It is also a good place to escape the winter cold for a season or two. Don't let these facts be discouraging. The point is, you will most likely go back to where you are living at some point, so do yourself a favor and don't be irrational when leaving your current city and end up making a decision you will later regret.

There are proper and improper ways to quit your job, many of which will be covered in this chapter. Resist the urge to skip forward to the next section and think about which way will be the best for you.

REASON TO QUIT — #6

Everybody stares at me when I drink margaritas at meetings.

Don't be disheartened. Though many newcomers only last a few short years on the island, people who stay for seven years or more often never leave. As the island starts to accept you, so do the natives. If you make it seven years in Key West you earn the title of Freshwater Conch. Who needs lucrative commercial endorsements anyway?

Way To Go?

Take This Job and Shove It:

How many hours have we spent on the company payroll fantasizing about the various ways we would tell our bosses where to stick it? Unfortunately it is only with age that we realize the best time to have done that was when we were seventeen and really didn't care what kind of references the pizza place would give.

Though sharing your true feelings about your place of employment, throwing your apron or a stack of inter-office memorandums at the boss, and walking out in a storm of dramatics and bravado with as much company property as you can fit in your pockets may feel good, in the long run it does not get you anywhere. You can scratch that job off when it comes to a reference, your former co-workers will probably bad-mouth you as they take on the additional work you left behind, and no matter how great you think you are, the place is going to survive just fine without you. Everyone is replaceable, and don't you forget it.

On the other hand, life is short and you will probably land on your feet. Make everyone see that you will not put up with anymore abuse; that you are deserving of a better life. For added effect you can

Fuzzy math? Duval Street is the longest street in the world. It's only a mile long, but runs from the Gulf of Mexico to the Atlantic Ocean.

wave your arms around like a spazzy child and tell everyone, "You can all go to hell! I'm going to Key West." They will be sure to remember you as the crazy rebel who left in a whirlwind: a legend in your own time.

But I Gave my Two Weeks:

So maybe you don't want to act all crazy and cause a big scene, but you do want to send a clear message to everyone that they suck. Try the pseudo two-week notice. Are you due vacation? Put in your vacation request and then submit your resignation the day you leave. Chances are they won't want you back at the end of your vacation, but you can still collect your check. If vacation time doesn't cover the 14-day period consider using sick days or personal days. Shady? Yes. But Key West is a sunny place for shady people. Send them a bumper sticker from the Green Parrot Bar.

Okay, Two More Weeks:

Give your two-week notice. This is really the best way to go. No sick days and no personal days. Be nice and calm. Tell your boss that you feel honored to have worked for him or her but you have a dream to follow and you must pursue it. Keep a door open by suggesting that you would love to work together again in the future. Be nice to all of your co-workers and tell them how much you will miss them. Play your cards right and you might get a nice going-away party complete with a framed photo of your work place signed by all of the employees. Stay forever in their thoughts by mailing tropical postcards every week.

Kitty Porn? Key West is famous for its cats with six or more toes. They may look cute, but the extra digits are a result of inbreeding. Scientists call them polydactyls. We call them one big happy family.

Absent Minded:

If uncertain as to your survival in Key West, consider asking your employer for a leave of absence. Tell them you need to take a few months off to find out where you are going with your life or that you are searching for your soul and need to take an adventure before you go postal. Use whatever excuse you think your employer will understand and be sure to say it is best for you and the company. It is cheaper for a lot of companies to allow this than it would be to train someone else to do your job. Tell them you'll be back in a few months and see what they say. Whether you return is up to you.

Slip Sliding Away

If none of the other options seems fitting, you could always try slipping out the back door. Don't tell anyone where you are going and "Poof!" disappear to the Keys never to be seen again. It happens every season in Key West.

Consider This

There are a few things to consider in the time between making your decision to quit and packing your bags to hit the road. Contain your excitement for a few moments and think about this:

$$$$$$:

Money can't buy you love, but it sure comes in handy if you need a plane ticket, gas money, hotel rooms, or first, last, security and a pair of Birkenstocks. Make sure you have a firm grip on your finances

Let it snow! The roof of the Custom House slopes at a 45-degree angle. The government required this so snow would slide off. Key West is one of the few frost-free cities in Florida.

before packing your bags and heading south. Everything is more expensive in the Keys, so budget a bit extra for your journey. Key West has a knack for eating away at your wallet no matter how much money you have. Captain Confucius say: Bring half the luggage and twice the money you think you need.

Bridges Burn:

All roads lead to Rome; only one road leads to Key West. The Overseas Highway has 42 bridges and burning any one of them would make it next to impossible to return to the mainland. The same can be said for the people you currently work with, your friends and your neighbors. Burning any one of them would make it next to impossible to return.

You might need your job back for starters, so keep in touch with the people in your business. Leaving on bad terms can spell certain disaster, and though you may think you don't need anybody now, your tune may change when you need references for a new job, a new apartment or a bank loan. You may be surprised at just how many people have ties to the Keys. They may have winter homes here, visit for vacation or pleasure, or sometimes just chat with a friend that lives in town. We guarantee you will see familiar faces on this 2 by 4 mile chunk of land and though you can run all you want, there is nowhere to hide.

It's All About Compassion.

When moving to Key West you can expect everyone to be insanely jealous. Sure, they will express how happy they are for you and tell you how much they would love to do that, but deep inside they will

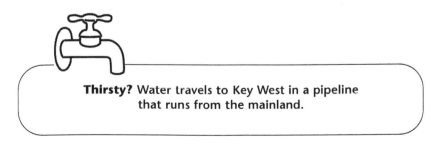

Thirsty? Water travels to Key West in a pipeline that runs from the mainland.

probably wish they were you and resent the fact they are not. It is important you avoid the temptation to gloat and realize that your friends' and family's feelings are at stake.

When leaving the boring job you have hated for the past few years, don't rub it in your co-workers' faces. They have to stay in that same boring, job day after day, week after week, while you live the life of sun, fun and exotic fruity drinks with umbrellas. (It's not always like that, but what they don't know can't hurt them.) Once you have settled in, invite them down for a weekend and the island will do the gloating for you. If you don't want them coming to visit – well, go ahead – a little gloating never hurt anybody.

What's The Plan, Stan?

The number one reason people don't make it in Key West is their complete lack of a plan. People come here to escape. Most convicts who escape from jail plan the escape well, but end up getting caught because they did not think about what they would do once they had gotten away.

Decide what you want out of your life in Key West before you get here. Write down your goals and actively pursue them every day. If your goal is to do absolutely nothing, that's great, but write it down in your plan. There is a good chance that your goals and ideas will evolve once you begin to implement them. Key West can be pretty cool like that. If you don't have any goals and can't be bothered to make a plan you should consider Miami. We have enough homeless people here and Miami has better shelters.

People in Key West love to complain. Our favorite joke: How many locals does it take to change a light bulb? Ten. One to change it and the other nine to complain about how much better it was before it changed.

Making
The Move
We're a movin' on up

What's the Story, Morning Glory?

*C*ongratulations on your newfound freedom. By now you should have quit your job and are either counting the days until your two weeks are up or are busy screening phone calls from your former co-workers telling you how much they appreciate the limb you have left them hanging from.

Now is the time to put the past behind you and focus on the future. The first thing you will need in Key West is a story. Why did you move here? Where did you come from? Why did you leave? How long have you been here? Get used to these questions now and be prepared to answer with a good story. About 3 million people come to Key West every year and seasoned locals have developed an advanced screening process. Your answers to the questions will determine where you stand and how quickly you acclimate.

People are first classified as either local or tourist. Once this crucial bit of information has been determined you will be subjected to further screening depending on your answer. The tourist will be treated cruelly or kindly based on situation and surrounding circumstances. (You will understand more once you have been here a few months.) Locals will be subject to further questioning to determine pack status.

How Long Have You Been Here?

We have mentioned before that Key West is not always an easy place to survive. Locals tend to wear their number of years in residence like a badge of honor. If you have only been here a few months or a couple of years, expect people to be less trusting. They may share a beer at the bar with you, and even invite you back to their home for a drink, but don't make the mistake of thinking you have a new friend who will be calling you tomorrow to say what a great time they had.

Don't take this as an insult. Remember that a large percentage of social activities in town revolve around drinking. You are likely to see this person again, but don't get upset if he or she doesn't recall your name or can't quite remember where they met you. Everybody is here for their own good time.

In some situations you may want to stretch the truth. If you only moved to town in the last week but have been vacationing here for years it is perfectly acceptable to say, "I've been coming here off and on for almost five years, but I just moved back last week."

Where Did You Come From?

This is nothing more than an attempt to find some common ground. Most people in Key West were not born here, so find a match and you are on your way to becoming a known member of the community. Shoot wide. Instead of saying you came from Chicago or another city, start with the state to improve your odds of bonding. If you have lived in multiple places, don't hesitate to throw them in. "Most recently Illinois, but I was born in Texas and grew up in Alaska." If no bond is made, expect to hear this next:

What Do You Do?

Even if you came from a dull and boring job this is a great opportunity to share a bizarre anecdote from your work experience. People in Key West thrive on weird stories. Failing an immediate common ground, you can expect a local to revert to selfish mode and see if there is anything you can do for them. If your skills or abilities don't meet any of their interests, abort the conversation or reverse the question to get them talking about themselves. (Authors warning: you may regret getting a Key West local to talk about themselves as many will never stop.)

Cuba Libre! Key West is closer to Havana than it is to Miami.

What Made You Come To Key West?

This is usually the fourth in a series of questions. If you have made it this far without the local losing interest, you are doing well. These may sound like simple questions, but the bottom line is this: there are a lot of people who come and go, life is short, and nobody wants to make friends with someone who is not going to be here very long – that's what acquaintances are for. Answer every question with conviction, originality and personality. Don't say you came here for the weather or the people. Everybody comes here for that. The more you stand out, the better you will be remembered. The better you are remembered, the more you will acclimate. As you acclimate, your love of Key West will grow, and before you know it you will be a Freshwater Conch with a nickname of your own.

Speaking of nicknames, people have enough trouble remembering first names, much less last. Nicknames are common. Key West has hundreds of captains who can't drive a boat, "The Cookie Lady," "Magic Frank," "The Rose Lady," "Tin Man," "Kwelvis," "Pirate Ned," "The Famous Mandy Bolen." The list goes on. More people would know who wrote this book if the title page said "Spooky Dave" and "Snow Ball." Give it some time and your name will come too.

Think about these things as you start preparing for your move. The next chapter will tell you everything you need to bring and some good advice on finding a place to live.

What To Bring?

Who are we to tell you what to bring? Famous Key West authors who are writing this book, that's who! Obviously we don't have a clue how many possessions (or lack of) you have to your name, and we are not here to have you ditch the precious stamp collection your grandfather left you on his deathbed. We do, however, want to tell you a bit about living conditions in Key West and give you some guidelines as to what you may or may not want to drag down here.

Whether coming for the season or the rest of your life, we recommend you pack light but smart. (Remember what Captain

Confucius said?) Think about what kind of move you will be making and consider the following factors.

Temperature:

It's hot, humid and tropical here. Temperatures have been known to drop into the mid 40's, but warm is the norm. Bring a couple of sweaters and one or two warm jackets, but leave the majority of your winter collection behind. You will do just fine most of the year in summer clothes.

Dress Code:

Key West Casual is the rule. The interpretation is up to you. Most restaurants will be happy to serve you provided you are wearing a shirt and shoes (and some kind of pants of course, shorts included.) Though it may seem strange at first, people conduct business in clothes that are comfortable. There are times for dressing up, so bring a few nice things, but formally-dressed people in the Keys are referred to as bride, groom or defendant. Ditch the tie collection and bring a few of your favorites. One dress suit should get you through the year just fine. Don't be too concerned about ironing, as the humidity will take care of most of it.

Furniture:

Know what you are moving into before you pack up all that furniture and make sure it will all fit. Bringing furniture is a good idea if you are purchasing a house for the simple reason that we don't have a lot of stores down here. Yes, you can get furniture, but selection is limited and you may be stuck paying too much for something you don't like.

Rebel yell? Key West was part of the Union during the Civil War.

On the flip side, people are moving out all the time and if diligent in your searches, you will find some pretty funky stuff for a good price at garage sales and thrift shops. If you get here and don't find anything to suit your taste you may need to take a trip to Miami or do some shopping on the Internet. Bring all of your prized possessions and you may have to sell some of them off because they just don't fit, which brings us to your next consideration.

Space:

We're not talking about that place NASA goes. We're talking about the amount of room you will have to store your stuff. If you move into a house, expect it to be smaller than the house you live in now. There will not be as many closets, there will be no basement, if you have an attic it will be small, and your yard will probably be a fraction of the size you are used to.

Apartment dwellers should not expect a cookie cutter complex designed with modern times in mind. Most apartments are nothing more than houses that have been chopped up into three or four units. This means minor details like storage have often been overlooked.

Consider these factors while packing up your belongings. Do you really need that mantle clock, the dress that is a size too small, eight sets of spare sheets? Would you really miss these items if you left them behind? Try using the one-year rule with clothes - if you have not worn them in a year get rid of them. Put together a garage sale if you want and raise some extra money for your trip down.

Speaking of trips, you really don't need your car when you get down here. A bike or a scooter will do fine and another space that is hard to come by is the parking space. Don't say we didn't warn you. More on that later.

REASON TO QUIT — #42

The alarm clock is evil; it must be punished.

Things to Bring

1. Wine Rack
2. Bicycle
3. Corkscrew
4. Hawaiian Shirt
5. Martini Shaker
6. Jimmy Buffett CDs
7. Little Cocktail Umbrellas
8. Beach Towel
9. Sunglasses
10. Aspirin

Things To Leave Behind

1. Alarm Clock
2. Winter Jacket
3. Suit and Tie
4. Ice Scraper
5. Car
6. Electric Blanket
7. In-Laws
8. Snow Shovel
9. Bad Attitude
10. Prozac

To Buy or Not to Buy? That is the Question.

Whether you are buying or renting, housing in Key West is very expensive. Both are achievable options, but figuring out which best suits you and finding the right place will take a bit of time. Plan wisely, as it will all be worth it once you're kicking back in your very own place called paradise.

E.T. Own Home:

Purchasing a house in Key West is very expensive but can also prove to be an excellent investment. This is one of the few tropical islands in the continental U.S. It is the southernmost city in the continental United States. A wise man (whose name we forget after years of living in the Keys) once said, "Buy land. They are not making any more of it." His advice adheres well in Key West.

The real estate market rose steadily for nearly thirty years. In 2006 it began to level out with the rest of the country, but the price for paradise is not cheap by any means. A friend of ours bought a house in 2000 for $190,000. Three years later, the property was appraised at $425,000. He sold the property for $850,000 in 2006 and moved to New York City to be on The Apprentice. Prices started dropping in 2007, but visitors still think they drank too much and are seeing an extra zero when they read the real estate listings. Call one of our friends in the real estate business to get the current scoop. You could be the next contestant on The Price is Right.

Room for Rent?

If you are only coming for the season, renting is probably your best option. This also works for many year-round residents who have bad credit or can't come up with a down payment on a house.

REASON TO QUIT — **#73**

I'm surrounded by idiots.

There are many avenues to take when looking for a place to live. You can go online at floridakeys.com or to the many local papers that have listings, the best one being The Citizen. We found the best way to find a place to rent is simply driving around town and looking for "For Rent" signs. They go quick so when calling around be prepared to go right away. Have all of your information prepared in advance: references, phone numbers and addresses. Also when renting a place in Key West be prepared to pay first, last and a security deposit to move in. This amounts to about three months rent. Not every rental place is like this; you might get lucky, but be prepared for the worst.

Rental Options:

If you have decided that renting is your best option, your next step is figuring out what to rent. There are a number of factors to consider such as money, people and availability.

There are plenty of houses and apartments available every year and they seem to go in and out of everybody's hands for one reason or another. Price is the first thing to consider. Sometimes utilities are included, other times they are not. Ask your landlord which utilities are included before signing a lease and check with the utility companies for annual averages on the property. Here is a list of general rent prices as of 2005.

- Room = $200 per week and up
- Studio = $900 a month and up
- 1 bedroom = $1,000-1,500 a month
- 2 bedroom = $1,400-$2,100 a month
- 3-4 bedroom house = $2,100 a month and up

All the buzz! Mosquitoes are so bad there is a Mosquito Control Board responsible for getting rid of them.

A small warning: Choose roommates carefully. There are all types of people down here: good and bad, daytime and nighttime, gay and straight, drinkers and non-drinkers. Some people party, some people don't. Avoid a sticky roommate situation by asking questions first. This island has a way of changing people for good and for bad. It spits out those it doesn't like, so be smart about making your rooming decisions as it can make or break your Key West experience.

Round, Round, Get Around:

Now that you have a place to call home it is time to figure out your mode of transportation. There are several other options to explore:

Cars:

Parking is at a premium and we have more cars than the island can handle. Most apartments and a good number of houses do not come with a parking space and you will be left to compete for the best spots. Parking meters are enforced heavily, seven days a week until midnight and run about one dollar an hour. Though your coach will come in handy for trips across town or excursions up the Keys, your best bet is to leave it parked and experience the island with some other forms of transportation.

Scooters:

People knock scooters and give them a bad rap. They are dangerous, noisy, and people zip around on them like they own the town. On the other hand, they are easy to park, fuel-efficient and most of all, fun. New ones run about $2,000, but used scooters can be found for considerably less. Lock your scooter up tight. Theft is not uncommon.

Ride Your Bike:

This is the preferred local transportation. Good for the environment, good for you, easy to get around and easy to park. The police can be strict on bicyclists so make sure you are equipped with lights at night and resist the temptation to go the wrong way down a one-way street. There is nothing more soothing than riding your goofy conch bike with big handle bars down the street during sunset. You won't remember how old you are. Captain Confucius say: He who does not lock his bike walks home.

Walk About:

One of the benefits of living on a small island is the ease of walking everywhere. Nothing is more than ten minutes away in Old Town and it provides a great opportunity to stop and chat with people. Another benefit is the ease of carrying a drink, as opposed to balancing it on your handlebars.

Skate Tough or Die:

Skateboards and roller blades are another way to get around the island, but be warned that neither of these is allowed down Duval Street, and skateboarding is illegal on any street. We don't recommend these modes of transportation for beginners. There is a skate park on Flagler Avenue.

Taxi, Taxi:

Though drinking is considered a sport in Key West, drinking and driving is not. Taxis are cheap; you can get pretty much anywhere on the island for less than $15. No matter what form of transportation you choose, call a taxi if you have been drinking. There are two major companies in town. Call 296-6666 or 292-0000. Both have bike racks and minivans for large groups if needed.

Pitter Patter. Tin roofs came into vogue after the great fire of 1886 when most of the wooden structures burned. They also provided a cleaner way to collect fresh rainwater.

Play Tourist
Enjoy it while you still can

Welcome to Key West. We're glad you're here, but before you get too wrapped up in a daily routine, take some time to smell the roses. There is an unwritten law in Key West that being a local is more prestigious than being a tourist. Soon, you too will be turning up your nose at the many great offerings our island has with the excuse, " I don't need to ride the Conch Train. I'm a local."

Do yourself a favor when you move here and take a week or two to play tourist. The following pages have just a few of the great tourist attractions worth checking out. Many of the attractions offer special deals for locals.

Original Ghost Tours: Key West has more ghosts per capita than any city in the United States. The Ghost Tour combines ghosts and history in a 90-minute walking tour. www.hauntedtours.com 305.294.9255

Audubon House: John James Audubon never lived here. The Audubon House was the home of Captain Geiger – the island's first Port Captain. Audio tours are offered daily and the gardens are a favorite for weddings and receptions. www.audubonhouse.com 305.294.2116

Butterfly World: Butterfly and Nature Conservatory: Walk among hundreds of living butterflies from around the world in a climate controlled, glass enclosed habitat. No "butterflies in your stomach" allowed. www.keywestbutterfly.com (305) 296-2988.

Need a drink? Before being connected to the mainland, people collected their water in a cistern, a cement receptacle for holding rainwater. Many of them have been turned into hot tubs and swimming pools.

Hemingway House: This was Ernest's home in Key West. It is just as famous for the cats that roam the property as for the writer. Do yourself a favor and remember the location of this one. We guarantee a tourist will ask directions for it one day soon. www.hemingwayhome.com 305.294.1136

Heritage House Museum: This house gives you a good feel of Key West in the good old days. Robert Frost stayed in the rear cottage. Call for tour information. 305.296.3573 www.heritagehousemuseum.org

Little White House: Every local should know Key West's presidential ties. Tour President Harry Truman's former residence and learn it all. www.trumanlittlewhitehouse.com 305.294.9911

Shipwreck Historeum: Impress tourists with your knowledge of Key West's maritime history. The Shipwreck Historeum is a good place to start. www.shipwreckhistoreum.com 305.292.8990

Mel Fisher Maritime Museum: Mel's the one who found the wreck of the Atocha – along with millions of dollars in sunken treasure. You can hear the story, see the treasure and learn more sea stories to impress tourists. www.melfisher.org 305.294.2633

Flagler Railroad Historeum: Learn all about the railroad that went to sea. Key West would not be what it is today without the railroad that once connected us to the mainland. www.flaglerstation.net

Key West Aquarium: Key West's version of SeaWorld. Pet a shark and

REASON TO QUIT ── #27

I'm starting to laugh at Al Roker's jokes.

get a hands-on education about our marine life. It will make your day. www.keywestaquarium.com 305.296.2051

East Martello Museum: This old fort was converted into a Key West history museum. Explore the Martello and discover tidbits from the island's past featuring everything from Indians to movies made in the Keys. 305.296.3913 www.kwahs.com/martello

Lighthouse Museum: Built in 1847, the lighthouse and adjacent keeper's quarters have been beautifully restored. www.kwahs.com/lighthouse 305.294.0012

Fort Zachary Taylor: In addition to being the locals' favorite beach, the state park has a fort that is worth exploring. Civil War reenactments are hosted here periodically. www.forttaylor.org 305.292.6713

Fort Jefferson/ Dry Tortugas National Park
: Plan a day trip to this historic fort located about 70 miles off Key West so you can explore the ruins and enjoy some of the best snorkeling around. The park can be accessed by boat or seaplane. Ferries can be contacted at www.fortjefferson.com
305.294.7009 or 292.6100

Conch Tour Train: Don't make the mistake of looking for train tracks around town. The Conch Tour train is on wheels, which offers a 90-minute tour with about 100 points of interest. The tour is an excellent way to increase your knowledge of local trivia. www.conchtrain.com 305.294.5161

REASON TO QUIT — #38

Staying home and watching "Scrubs" is my idea of a wild night.

Old Town Trolley Tour: No tracks here either. The trolley is similar to the Conch Train, but allows you to get off at different stops to enjoy the nearby attractions. www.trolleytours.com/keywest 305.296.6688

Ripley's Believe It or Not: A museum of the wild, wacky and unusual from around the world. Ripley's has odditoriums across the United States, but the Key West location features many exhibits unique to our island. www.ripleyskeywest.com 305.293.9939

Pirate Soul: Check out the largest and most authentic collection of pirate artifacts under one roof. Swing by the Rum Barrel while you are there and you might meet Key West's favorite modern day pirate, Pat Croce. 305.292.1113 www.piratesoul.com

Snorkeling: You may have been snorkeling before, but Key West offers a very different experience with our coral reef. Imagine fish, hundreds of fish, in all different colors, shapes and sizes. You may see sharks, rays, sea turtles and lobster. There is no shortage of companies offering trips to the reef, so ask around and find the one that best suits your needs.

Sunset Sails: Your only chance of experiencing a green flash is at sea. This rare occurrence can only be seen on the water as the sun sets. The island is home to a number of classic schooners and sailing ships, perfect for a romantic evening getaway. Remember that each boat only offers one sunset sail per evening. Only a tourist would think otherwise.

First last call. Liquor license No. 1 was issued to a bar on Duval Street called Pepe's, which is now known as Rick's.

Other attractions: Like people, attractions come and go in this town. By the time you read this book, some of the above attractions may be gone and new ones will have taken their place. When planning your activities, pick up the local tourist guides and look through the different brochure racks to make sure you get the most out of your first week in town.

We know what some of you are thinking: "These attractions sound great, but I just put down first and last month's rent and a security deposit on an apartment. I'm not made of money like you successful authors are and you are crazy if you think I can afford to do all of that."

Relax. Plan to do the attractions over time and start with some of the great free things that Key West has to offer. As a local you are obligated to keep these free things a secret from the tourists. We need their money.

Key West Cemetery: Our cemetery has more than 100,000 residents and features above ground burials. See if you can find the grave marker that reads, "I told you I was sick." If you need help you can find guide maps at local bookstores. The cemetery is open from sunrise to sunset, but most true locals have taken a midnight stroll amongst the graves to test their spirit. All have survived, though some end up in jail for trespassing.

Historic Memorial Sculpture Garden: Some locals will refer to this as the "Pez Garden" due to the similarities between the statues and the famous candy dispensers. The garden is located near Mallory Square off Duval Street, and offers excellent insight into the lives of people

REASON TO QUIT — #41

Everyone keeps asking me when I'll get a real job.

who played a significant role in shaping Key West.

St. Paul's Episcopal Church: Key West is home to many beautiful churches, but our favorite is St. Paul's on the corner of Duval and Eaton streets. The stained glass is exquisite and this is the oldest non-Roman Catholic Church in the state of Florida.

Catch of the Day: Garrison Bight Marina is located just off North Roosevelt Boulevard (locals leave out the North Roosevelt part and just call it "the boulevard") on Palm Avenue. This is the spot where most of the sport-fishing boats dock. You will be amazed at the spectacle as the fishermen show off their catch, clean the fish before your eyes, and toss the scraps aside for the other fish and pelicans to fight over. Most boats start returning in the late afternoon.

Sunset: The sunset is free, but Mallory Square is not the only place to watch it. Take in the best view from the top of the Crowne Plaza La Concha or head out to the community college for a romantic sunset from the Oriental Torii Garden.

The list of free things to do is only limited by your imagination. Enjoy people-watching on Duval Street, ride your bike, explore the incredible architecture the city has to offer or take one of the free tours listed in Sharon Wells' walking and hiking guide. Explore our parks and beaches or just walk through town. You will soon realize that every journey through Key West has the potential to become an adventure.

Monkey on your back? Key West has its own Sasquatch known as the Skunk Ape. People have claimed to see it running through the mangroves.

Honey, I'm Home

Your Personal
Key West Welcome Wagon

Got Gas?

If not, you better get cooking. In addition to gas you will need to sign up for water, electricity and all the other goodies that turn your house into a home. Learn from our mistakes and go into each utility with identification, a copy of your lease and some cash to leave a deposit; remember, you're new in town and we don't trust you yet.

To make your first days in paradise a little more bearable, most utilities are listed below. The smart local says, "Call them first and find out what you need." The stupid local says, "A few days without running water never hurt nobody."

Keys Energy Service: 1001 James Street, 305.295.1000

Most of our electricity is purchased from the mainland. When the wires have problems it is not uncommon for the entire island to lose power. Because prices fluctuate so much there is a fuel adjustment charge that will appear on your bill each month. Expect it to soar in the summer months. When the power is out on the traffic lights, the intersection becomes a four way stop; you may know this, but no one else in Key West does, so proceed with caution.

Florida Keys Aqueduct Authority: 1100 Kennedy Drive, 305.296.2454

Miami is notorious for its poor water quality. Take Miami water and send it down an additional 200 miles of pipeline and you have Key West water. Yes, it is safe to drink, but as science is finding new reasons to die on a daily basis, consider calling the next number on the list.

Zephyrhills Drinking Water: 1.800.950.9398

REASON TO QUIT

Water cooler stories just aren't the same since
"Seinfeld" went off the air.

Suburban Propane: 726 Catherine Street, 305.296.2411
Columbia Propane: 1718 N. Roosevelt Blvd., 305.294.3527

There is a good chance your water heater or stove runs on propane. Don't worry- it's cheap, and you don't have to take your tank in to be filled. Suburban will come to your house about once a month and refill your outdoor tank. During your refill, 27 locals will curse them for blocking the road.

Waste Management: 305.296.8297

Getting trashed? Waste management will pick up your empty beer bottles, as well as all the other garbage you put in your big green can. Key West has mandatory recycling, which is done in the blue containers. Think roosters are bad? Wait until you are awakened by the sound of smashing beer bottles at 5:30 a.m. Just remember, it's good for the environment.

AT&T: 305.780.2355

Key West will soon fall victim to 10-digit dialing. Lucky for us, ma is always there to make us feel better; Ma' Bell that is. Key West is blessed with excellent phone service, so go ahead, reach out and touch someone – just make sure they are of age.

Comcast Cable: 305.292.8376

Forget about cheating the cable companies by using the old rabbit ears and getting by on network television. We don't get network

Luck of the English? Conch shells are good luck unless you bring them into your house. The bad luck that follows is know as the conchs' revenge! A conch shell was presented as a gift to Queen Elizabeth. Judging by tabloid reports, she took it into the Palace.

television in Key West except through the cable companies. AT&T offers a variety of packages from basic to digital, but that won't help you much when they get scooped up by another telecommunications giant and change their name and phone numbers in the merger.

Internet: . It took a little while, but the Florida Keys finally pulled out of the Dark Ages and hopped on the high speed Internet train. DSL service available from Bellsouth and Comcast provides high speed connections. Or visit one of our many internet cafes

Car Stuff:	Drivers Licenses	Vehicle Registration
	3439 South Roosevelt Blvd.	1200 Truman Ave
	305-293-6338	305-295-5000

If you need anything else, check the Yellow Pages, you lazy bum!

Proud Mary Keeps on Learnin'

Educational standards are an important concern when relocating if you have children. We don't have children, and chances are, if you are quitting your job and moving to Key West, you don't have any either. (At least none that you are bringing with you.) If you do, this is when we say, "Sorry." Below is a list of schools you can check out on your own. Talk to a realtor and they can point you in the right direction for finding out the data you are looking for. Our book is only 128 pages and we'll be damned if we're wasting any more space on something as stoopid as skool.

Florida Keys Community College
509 W. College Rd.
305-296-9081

Key West High School
2100 Flagler Ave.
305- 293-1549

Poinciana Elementary
1212 14th Street
305-293-1601

Lighthouse Christian Academy
5580 Macdonald Ave
305-292-5587

Sigsbee Elementary
Sigsbee Military Base
305-294-1861

Horace O'Bryant Middle School
1105 Leon St.
305-296-5628

Grace Lutheran School
2713 Flagler Ave.
305-296-8262

Mary Immaculate Star of the Sea
700 Truman Ave.
305-294-1031

Montessori Elementary Charter
1221 Varela St.
305-294-5302

Glynn Archer Elementary
1302 White St.
305-293-1609

Gerald Adams Elementary
5855 W. College Rd.
305-293-1906

Key West Organizations

Key West Garden Club
West Martello Towers
305-294-1545

Key West Association of Realtors
3422 Duck Ave.
305-296-1504

Key West Lions Club
2545 N. Roosevelt Blvd.
305-294-5853

Botanical Garden Society
College Road, Stock Island
305-296-1504

Sail and Power Squadron
5205 College Rd.
305-294-0096

Art & Historical Society
281 Front Street
305-295-6616

REASON TO QUIT — #97

If I have one more conversation about office politics I'll
throw myself down the stairs.

Key West Woman's Club	Chamber of Commerce
319 Duval Street.	402 Wall Street
305-294-2039	305-294-2587
Silver Slipper Club	Literary Foundation
305-294-7879	305-293-9291
V.F.W. Post 3911	The Business Guild
225 Elizabeth St.	728 Duval Street.
305-294-9968	305-294-4603
Gay and Lesbian Community Center	Innkeepers Association
1075 Duval Street.	922 Caroline Street
305-292-3223	305-295-1334
Alcoholics Anonymous	American Cancer Society
305-296-8654	305-594-4363
Big Brothers/Big Sisters	Monroe Assoc. for Retarded Citizens
305-294-9891	305-294-9526

That Time of the Month?

One of the great things about Key West is the incredible number of festivals, street fairs, parades, and parties we have throughout the year. Changes of season we may not have, and most residents have some degree of trouble remembering the day of the week, but you can always tell what time of the year it is based on the mood of the town and the event we're celebrating. (What an island!) Enjoy the next few pages as we take you on a month-by-month journey of life on the rock. Like sands through the hourglass, these are the days of our lives.

September

We know what you are thinking. Calendars are supposed to start with January. Now is the time to get it through your brain that Key West is different and for some mysterious reason, September is when our year seems to begin.

In September you can expect an average high temperature of 88.9 degrees with an average low of 78.8. Expect about 6 inches of rain, most in short doses of one hour or less.

September is typically the slowest month of the year as far as tourism is concerned. As tourism is the island's major industry, this is the month you can expect businesses to close either permanently or temporarily, unemployment rates to rise, and service industry employees to tighten their belts and pray they can cover their bills until Fantasy Fest in October.

A large sector of our population plans in advance for the slow times and takes an extended vacation, while those who remain can enjoy events such as Womenfest. This weeklong lesbian festival features plenty of girl parties, theater performances, art shows, bar specials and other activities all about women. There is also the Poker Run – a charitable biker event that spans the Keys raising money for local charities, ending with a big bash in the streets of Key West. What a sight to see thousands of bikes lining Duval Street from the Gulf to the Atlantic. Don't forget your earplugs. For the sportfishing enthusiasts there is the Mercury Outboard S.L.A.M. Fishing Tournament, a celebrity light-tackle event where all proceeds go to finding a cure for cystic fibrosis.

General Mood of Town: Slow and Low.
Overall Rating: 2 1/2 coconuts.
Local Advice: If you're not a lesbian, a biker, or a lesbian biker this is a good month to visit the family.
Biggest Threat: Can you say hurricane?

October

Everybody gets excited about October, but then they realize it is pretty much like September until Fantasy Fest hits at the end of the month. Fantasy Fest is the biggest party of the year – our own little Mardi Gras complete with parades, body painting, beads, boobs and booze.

This is also when friends you never knew existed call you out of the blue to see if they can crash on your couch for a few days. Don't be surprised if they forget to mention the friends they will bring, the new friends they will return with each night, and the vomit stains they will leave on your carpet.

The event gets a nice warm-up with the mostly local Goombay Celebration. This two-day celebration in Bahama Village is filled with Caribbean music, food, arts and crafts, food, booze and food. Did we mention the food? Come with an appetite.

If you are searching for a new apartment, get going in the early part of the month. As the snowbirds start to migrate, the best nests fill up quickly and you will be left sucking an egg. Don't rush out to get that winter jacket quite yet. The average high temperature is 83 degrees with a low of 74. You can expect about 5.8 inches of rain as well as a hurricane scare or two.

> **General Mood:** Premature Ejubilation.
> **Overall Rating:** Weeks 1-3, 4 coconuts.
> Week 4, 9 1/2 coconuts (and a few bananas)
> **Local Advice:** Don't blow your wad – there are still 55 shopping days until Christmas.
> **Biggest Threat:** Injuries caused by body painting, beads, boobs, and booze – or arrest

REASON TO QUIT — **#55**

I spend my free time reading self-help books.

November

The mood in November is greatly influenced by the success of our Fantasy Fest celebration. While many residents spend the first part of the month recovering from a Goliath-sized hangover, others seek out a good attorney to get their indecent exposure charges dropped. Most of the business community looks toward the holiday season as they face the harsh reality that the town is going to be slow until Christmas.

This is the time of year when you can identify the people who have been out of the snow for too long. While the high temperatures average somewhere around 83 degrees, the low dips below 70 to a frigid 69.7. Anything below 70 degrees is considered an excuse to get out the winter clothes that hang in the back of the closet 359 days of the year. Mid-November is when locals stop praying and making sacrifices to the Hurricane Gods and give thanks that we were spared yet another year. Our average rainfall drops to just 2.8 inches.

The powerboat races come to town. Those who don't watch the races can still have a good time in the downtown area looking at the huge boats and cracking jokes about what the racers might be compensating for. Also look for the Pirates in Paradise Festival.

Thanksgiving in Key West is a special time. This is when you realize you and your group of new friends are something special – you are family. You will find them to be people from all over the world, of all different cultures, ethnicities, flavors and sexual preferences getting together and cooking a feast to celebrate what we are all thankful for- living in Key West.

General Mood: How many more shopping days until Christmas?

Overall Rating: 5 coconuts, 1 turkey

Local Advice: If you don't have friends, this month sucks.

Biggest Threat: Getting beat up by a powerboat driver for making fun of his privates or augmented girlfriend.

December

Fla la la la la, la la la la. (That's a Florida joke, folks.) Welcome to the holiday season in Key West. You may not have family here, and there is definitely no snow, but Key West has a unique way of stepping up to the plate and hitting a home run when it comes to the holidays. Even God knows it's a damn good time.

Not a day goes by without some kind of holiday party. This is when every bar, restaurant, company and organization celebrates, and if you are in the know, they want you there. Every weekend is a Christmas bash at someone's house and you will find yourself hard-pressed to have to pay for a drink.

Though the weather outside ain't frightful, the season is still delightful. Average high, 74 degrees. Average low a chilling 65.8. Don't dream of a white or a wet Christmas; we only get about 2.9 inches of rain.

To kick off the season right check out the Holiday Parade down Truman Ave and Duval Street. Floats parade through Old Town celebrating the holiday season and there is even a Santa Claus. Word has it he was sick of freezing his buns off at the North Pole, quit his job and moved here (wise man that he is.) It could be just a rumor, but he did buy a copy of our book last year.

To really get into the holiday spirit Key West style one of the coolest things to see this time of year is the lighted boat parade. This local favorite features boats of all shapes and sizes cruising through the Historic Seaport lit up and decorated for the holidays.

Christmas Day is special to anyone in the tourism industry. This is truly the day that marks the beginning of our busy season. Every

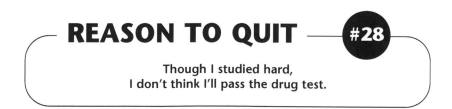

REASON TO QUIT — **#28**

Though I studied hard,
I don't think I'll pass the drug test.

hotel is filled to capacity, restaurants have lines out the doors, and parking spaces downtown are non-existent. People know there will be a steady stream of money for the next few months giving us all a reason to be happy in the New Year. (Author's note: money does not buy happiness.)

Finish December off right and get crazy with the Key West New Year's Eve Celebrations. The Southernmost City celebrates New Year's Eve with a fireworks display (when the city budget can afford it) and some droppings that rival the ball in New York. In the Key West tradition of uniqueness, a drag queen is lowered from a giant, red high-heeled shoe on the 800 block of Duval. Talk about a town with sole, er...soul. Sloppy Joe's drops a giant conch shell, which has rapidly become a world-famous event and the Schooner Wharf Bar lowers a pirate wench from a ship's mast.

> **General Mood:** 'Tis the season to be jolly.
> **Overall Rating:** 9 coconuts...and a partridge in a pear tree.
> **Local Advice:** Eat for free, drink for free, and be merry.
> **Biggest Threat:** Holiday hangovers and being squashed by a high-heeled shoe with a drag queen inside laughing gaily.

Ain't superstitious! The ceilings of porches on conch houses are painted blue to keep evil spirits away. It also works for wasps and mosquitoes.

January

Ponce de Leon came by Key West looking for the Fountain of Youth. He may have stayed longer had he visited in January.

There is something invigorating about the first month of the year on The Rock. People who have survived the slow times stand tall like proud flowers who survived the winter cold. A youthful energy fills the air. Ironically, January is actually the coldest month of the year with a low of 64.5 degrees and a high of only 75.8. Rainfall takes another slight drop with only two inches expected.

As the new year dawns it is not uncommon for people to cut back on their vices and work toward personal improvement. Key West is much the same, and January boasts more non-drinking events than most of the other months combined.

Key West's theater season begins in January with incredibly talented actors and actresses performing at The Waterfront Playhouse, Red Barn Theater and Tennessee Williams Fine Arts Center in Key West. They produce a number of great plays, musicals, dance ensembles, as well as special guest performances. Old Island Days is another cultural event that celebrates our island's roots with garden tours, conch shell blowing competitions and more.

To ensure a sobering month, we always kick off the New Year with the Key West literary seminar. It features workshops, panel discussions with distinguished writers and other adventures in the literary world. This is traditionally held the first week of the month, as once Hemingway is mentioned everyone screws their resolutions and heads straight to Sloppy Joe's.

General Mood: Sobering but productive
Overall Rating: 7.5 coconuts
Local Advice: A month on the wagon will do you some good.
Biggest Threat: Bruises from falling off wagon

February

February is unique in that it is the only month void of any major festivals or events. Why, you ask? The answer is quite simple. It is so friggin' cold everywhere else in the United States that we don't have to do anything to lure people here. Those who think highly of themselves will tell you we are in "the height of season," but they are jackasses. As we mention elsewhere in this book, there is no season, just busy times and slow times.

Temperatures start to warm up, and though the low stays around 66 degrees, our average high is close to 76. Rainfall drops just below 2 inches, but no one complains because we all have more money to pay for the higher water bills.

This is the time of year we all realize why we quit our jobs to move here. The weather is nice, the locals are nice, the tourists are nice and the money is nice. This is the stuff postcards are made of. As there are no festivals to attend, we recommend you sit back, grab an ice cold one and thank God you're not living in Buffalo. (Editors note: The authors have nothing against Buffalo except the temperature in February.)

General Mood: It's all good.
Overall Rating: 9 coconuts, but who's counting?
Local Advice: Enjoy it while it lasts. This is why you came.
Biggest Threat: Funeral in Buffalo.

Sublime? Santeria is Key West's version of voodoo. It originated in Yoruba, Nigeria. It is a mixture of voodoo, superstition and Roman Catholicism. It is still practiced today.

March

If you like binge drinking and hard-bodied teenagers, Duval Street in March is the place to be. College kids from all over the country come to Key West to squeeze a year's worth of partying into one short Spring Break. A common saying that originated during Spring Break and has gradually spread throughout the rest of the year is, "What happens on the rock stays on the rock."

Key West really recaptures its youth in this month that separates the young and the young at heart from the old and the grouchy. All-you-can-drink specials dominate the bars, beeping scooters rule the streets and the early morning crowing of roosters is dulled by the sounds of drunken youth stumbling home after one of the best nights of their lives.

Before you go getting upset at the youth gone wild, remember that you were young once too. (Key West fun fact: Quit Your Job and Move to Key West co-author David Sloan was arrested for underage drinking during his first Key West Spring Break in March, 1988.)

If this sort of debauchery is not quite your speed there are many other activities to float your boat such as the Historic Seaport Music Festival and the Annual Conch Shell Blowing Contest. People of all ages compete to see who can blow the best conch. (The shell, not the native, you sick and perverted thing.) This may be the only chance you get to blow a shell and win a prize.

Temperatures in March are perfect for bikinis and swim trunks. Expect an average high of close to 81 degrees and an average low of about 70 degrees. Rainfall is nearly nonexistent at 1.7 inches. Enjoy the sun and the view!

General Mood: I feel like I'm 19 again!
Overall Rating: 8.5 bikini-clad coconuts.
Local Advice: Sixteen will get you twenty.
Biggest Threat: Seeing your younger sister (or daughter) in a wet T-shirt contest.

April

April Fools! Oh, wait, all the fools are up north wondering how much longer winter will last. April is a great month in Key West. We've made it through winter without seeing snow, partied hard for Fantasy Fest, celebrated New Year's Eve and celebated (haven't we? That's not a typo) Spring Break. Everyone has worked their tails off to make the tourists happy for the past several months, so now it is time to reward ourselves.

There are a few special events in the Keys during April. The Conch Republic Independence Celebration takes place in mid-April and celebrates our secession from the United States in 1982. The week-long festivities include parades and parties, but culminate in the Great Land-Sea Battle where the Conch Republic Army – that's us, buster – engages in battle with the United States Navy using weapons such as stale loaves of Cuban bread, soggy conch fritters, rotten tomatoes and other produce. Picture a giant food fight on the water and you have the Great Battle.

For you health nuts, or at least those who try to be a health nut down here, there is also the Seven-Mile Bridge Run. Guess how long it is? Though the event does not take place in Key West, it is a big thing for the Keys. Even if you don't participate it would be wise to keep track of the event. People trying to leave the island on this day will be greeted by a large traffic jam as the bridge is closed for the race. Don't sweat the run. Average high, 82 degrees. Average low, 70 degrees. The rainfall is minute at 1.8 inches.

General Mood: We seceded where others failed.
Overall Rating: 9 coconuts and a few rotten tomatoes.
Local Advice: Even rotten tomatoes can bruise.
Biggest Threat: Rotten tomatoes.

May

May marks the official end of the season that doesn't really exist. As the weather becomes beautiful in the northern states, snowbirds leave their nests to return home, hotel rates drop, and tourism takes a slight dip, making it possible to walk down Duval Street without much difficulty. (Depending, of course, on how much you have had to drink.) The town is still busy, but no longer packed to the brim.

This is when a lot of locals will have their family and friends from out of town come visit. Hotels and guesthouses offer some excellent deals, making the trip more affordable as most apartments are too small to accommodate more than a few extra guests. Now is also a good time to play tourist. Head out with your friends and take a ride on the Conch Train or enjoy a barbeque at Fort Zachary Taylor. Check out some of the museums and rediscover what makes Key West such a cool place. As the year slips by it is easy to get in the habit of ragging on the tourist attractions. Getting out there and doing them will make you realize how much fun they actually are.

Look for some outdoor concerts this month. The weather is amazing with an average high of 86 degrees and an average low of 76 degrees. It is the perfect time to go out fishing, get on the snorkel boats, hit the beach and get in the water. Remind yourself why you're here. It's your island!

General Mood: Hooray! Hooray! The month of May! Outdoor loving begins today! (Isn't that right, Mr. Madison?)

Overall Rating: 8 coconuts

Local Advice: Check water quality advisories before you get in the water.

Biggest Threat: Fecal coliform growin' in the water.

June

Hot time, summer in the city – back of my neck's getting burnt and pretty. This is your last chance to really appreciate the island's weather before the heat and humidity get so intense you find yourself making excuses to hide inside and worship the people at GE for making air-conditioners affordable. The weather also provides an excellent excuse to indulge yourself with a Corona at 11:00 a.m. Schools let out and the families start heading to town bringing a deluge of children and campers to the island.

Warm water and calm seas bring the powerboat races back again and the town comes alive with the excitement they always bring. Head-turning, ear-burning super boats, as well as other classes race in this event.

On the other side of the coin is the Key West Theater Festival. Theater people from all around come to the southernmost city and show off their thespian skills for the folks that come to watch and participate in this nationally-known event. Can you handle the drama?

The Cuban-American Heritage Festival is another favorite with locals. Traditional Cuban food, story-telling, cultural and educational events are celebrated and the world's largest conga line dances it's way down Duval Street.

Enjoy a balmy high of 88 degrees and a low of 79. Expect about 4 inches of rain as hurricane season looms around the corner.

General Mood: Living la vida loca!
Overall Rating: 7 conga-nuts
Local Advice: Take conga lessons before joining the line.
Biggest Threat: No air-conditioning

REASON TO QUIT — #16

If it's good enough for Buffett and Hemingway,
it's good enough for me, damn it!

July

"It's 98 degrees in the shade." Nothing short of a cold beer will cool you down this time of the year. It's hot, it's sticky and it's time for the Hemingway Days Festival. This celebration of the author's work and life includes readings, poetry slams, tours of his old stomping grounds and the world famous Hemingway look-alike contest. Who wouldn't love a town with hundreds of 60-year-old men with white beards getting drunk and telling stories at Sloppy Joe's?

The Lorian Hemingway Short Story Competition celebrates writing at its best and presents cash prizes as well as bragging rights to writers of the top three stories.

Key West celebrates the Fourth of July with a bang that usually includes fireworks. There are always several parties and backyard barbeques as the town fills up with tourists from Miami ready to wave their flags (and a few sheets) in the wind.

If you're sick and tired of the literary scene, head down to the annual Tropical Fruit Fiesta. This event features more fruit than Carmen Miranda's hat, all available to taste or purchase.

Curious about the temperature in July? It's hot! The average high this time of year is a sweltering 91 degrees with an average low of 81 degrees. Sounds pretty good until you throw in the humidity. Leave the iron unplugged this July and expect to have a bad hair month. You will swear it is at least 110 degrees out there.

General Mood: Feeling hot, hot, hot!

Overall Rating: 6 sweaty coconuts

Local Advice: No "banana in your pocket" jokes at the fruit festival. They don't think it's funny. (Trust us on this one.)

Biggest Threat: Getting beaten up by drunk Hemingway look-a-likes.

August

Planning on visiting friends up north? Do it in August. Nothing happens here. Really. Nothing. It's hot, the kids are going back to school, the town is dead, and the ocean is like bath water.

The average temperature reaches a high of 89 degrees and a low of 78 degrees. The humidity is so thick you cannot leave the house without picking up a lovely layer of sweat.

This is a good time to tell you about hurricanes. To some they are cyclones with heavy rain and winds exceeding 75 mph, but to most of us in Key West they are another excuse for a party. You should take some time to read up on hurricanes and become familiar with the threat they pose. The phone book has a section dedicated to these storms to help you implement a hurricane plan, but we will tell you what really happens in Key West.

When a storm looks like it may head our way everyone flocks to the stores and you will be hard-pressed to find items such as plywood, batteries, candles and bottled water. The news crews will come to town and show footage that sends everyone into a frenzy and the county may issue a mandatory evacuation. Most people will choose to ignore the evacuation and shack up to party with friends. We have been fortunate so far.

General Mood: The answer, my friend, is blowin' in the wind.
Overall Rating: A humid 4.5 coconuts.
Local Advice: Stock up on batteries and water in July.
Biggest Threat: Category 5 Hurricane.

Flagler's Folly? People laughed when Flagler proposed running a railroad to Key West from the mainland. It has since been converted to the Overseas Highway and transports nearly 90 percent of our visitors. Who's laughing now?

Where The Wild Things Are
Local Hangouts

You will quickly learn that, in Key West, things are always changing. New businesses open every day and sadly, many close. Having said this, you will want to get out and go to the bars and restaurants that your fellow locals visit. Though these are sure to change over time, in the next few pages we will share some of our favorites, in hopes they will be around for a long time. Check them out for yourself and you might meet a couple of famous Key West authors.

Drinking Holes:

Hog's Breath – This local and tourist favorite has been around for years and is a staple of the Key West nightlife. Great live music from local musicans and national acts.

Green Parrot – Cheap beer, good live rock & blues, and skeeball. No sniveling.

Lazy Gecko – One of the only locals bar on lower Duval Street. Girls dance on the bar and the sandwiches are big.

Louie's Backyard After Deck – Not all the locals can afford to eat here, but we sure like to go for a nightcap on the deck. Best view on the island with a drink in your hand. Very romantic.

Grand Vin – Fun place to get a bottle of wine and chill out. Fair prices. Cool bartenders. Good view of Duval from the big front porch.

Rick's upstairs- Rick's has added a special bar for locals complete with a giant aquarium and a bird's eye view of the bands at Durty Harry's.

Scandal? Key West is home to the Clinton Square Market, the Lewinski building and several cigar shops.

Virgilio's – Jazz, rock, sometimes a DJ and the best martinis on the island. Good local hangout on the weekdays. A little crowded on weekends.

Rum Barrel – Rum, pirates, a great deck, awesome bands and Pat Croce! What more could you want from a bar.

Bone Island Bob's – This funky little joint on Greene Street off Duval serves as a convenience store, coffee shop and bar. This a prime spot to kick back with a drink and watch the world go by or stock up on your beer, butts and booty. Enjoy the local prices.

Finnegan's Wake – Small Irish joint near the wharf. Great Guinness and the best potato-leek soup this side of Dublin. Expect the bar to be filled to the brim with transplants from Ireland and England.

Schooner Wharf – This is a great local bar for tourists. It is right on the water and captures the feeling of old Key West. Tell Evalena Chris and David said hello.

Restaurants:

There are many restaurants that line Duval Street. You will find a decent, slightly over-priced meal at almost every one. There are some out of the way restaurants offering a great meal for a local price. Here is a list of our local dining favorites.

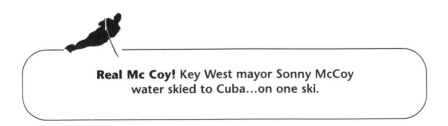

Real Mc Coy! Key West mayor Sonny McCoy
water skied to Cuba...on one ski.

Seven Fish – Tucked away on a small side street in Old Town, this eclectic place seats about 20 people with a few coveted bar stools. You have a selection of – you guessed it, seven fish. All seven of them are worth a try.

Banana Café – located at the southern end of Duval Street, this French café is a favorite for the breakfast they serve until 3 p.m. Great crepes, omelets and coffee. You see all the late-nighters getting up to start their day around 2 p.m.

Mr. Z's – Steps away from Duval Street, this cheese steak and pizza joint has quickly became a local favorite for its great eats and Philly Flare Cheap beer and an entertaining staff make for never a dull moment. We highly recommend stopping here for lunch, dinner or stumble by for a late night snack.

Santiago's Bodega – Located in the heart of Bahama Village, this eclectic restaurant is open for both lunch and dinner serving a variety of tapas-style bits for you to enjoy. Off the beaten path and not your average bear, this joint has become a local favorite.

Sandy's Café a.k.a M&M Laundry – Off the beaten path on White Street past Truman Avenue. This tiny Cuban deli window shop is located in a laundromat. It has some of the best Cuban mix sandwiches and breakfast burritos you will find, as well as the best coffee on the island. Talk about strong coffee – the guys behind the counter never stop cleaning. Late-night people love Sandy's as they open around 5:30 a.m. everyday.

Full of Ship? Cruise ships are supposed to leave Mallory Square before sunset so as not to block the view. Violating vessels are fined.

El Siboney - Talk about some great Cuban food. Located on Catherine Street, the traditional Cuban cooking is guaranteed to put the Cayo in your Hueso. Try it - you'll love it.

The Cafe - This mostly vegetarian restaurant will please both carnivores and leaf eaters with some of the best vegetarian cuisine on the island. Great atmosphere, amazing food and a wait staff with interesting names.

Milk, Milk, Lemonade, Around the Corner Coffee's Made

Flamingo Crossing - A favorite ice cream shop that serves homemade ice cream and other frozen treats. Indulge in a cone or cup around 9 p.m. while sitting at an outdoor table watching the action go by. Luckily enough, our favorite wine bar, Grand Vin, is right next door in case you need to put a little more flavor on your palate.

Coffee and Tea House - Located at the end of Duval near the Southernmost Point, this charming little place has a great atmosphere to drink coffee, enjoy a conversation, read a book, or play dominoes. Great for mornings on the porch.

Wayne's Lemonade Stand - Located on the corner of Fleming and Duval right next to Fast Buck Freddie's, Wayne serves up the best hot dogs and freshest lemonade on the island.

REASON TO QUIT — #12

The closest I've come to being surrounded by water is sitting in my bathtub.

Local Secrets

The longer you live here the more things you will find to do. Here are some of our favorite local secrets for you to check out. We can't tell you all of ours (if we did, they wouldn't be secrets) so be sure to find some of your own.

White Street Pier – Located at the end of White Street, the pier jets out into the ocean providing a wonderful place to watch the sunrise. Locals meet to chat with their neighbors as the sun goes down and the pier proves to be an inexpensive snorkeling alternative to the reef.

The Top at La Concha – This is the tallest building in town and provides a breathtaking view of the island. Sunset is the most popular time to take in the views and grab a cold one, but the observation deck is open all day.

Bayview Park – Tennis courts, basketball courts and the occasional bums drinking in the gazebo. Great place to toss a Frisbee or just relax.

Little Hamaca Park – The only secluded park on the island. A great walk or bike ride through the mangroves and Key West nature. As this area is secluded, it sometimes attracts less reputable people, so don't send your kids alone.

Dog Park – Near White Street Pier, a section of park has been gated off for the dogs. It is quite the social scene for the dogs and the owners.

Fidel Castro once visited Key West and stayed in a room on Truman Avenue.

The City Pool - Tucked away in Bahama Village, this giant public pool is free and never crowded. A great place to go for a swim or play silly pool games.

Bocce Courts - Located at the end of White Street by Higgs Beach, these courts are a great place to toss a couple balls back and forth or toss back a couple beers. Leagues play a few nights a week, so get involved.

The Nasty Burger Joint - We're not sure of the actual name for the place, but it's across from Blue Heaven on Petronia Street. There are no set hours or days, but if it's open, stop in and get a Nasty Burger. So big, so juicy, so gosh darn good you will wish they were open every-day.

Nancy's Secret Garden - This hidden jewel is tucked away at the end of Free School Lane, which stems off Simonton Street near Southard. It is a tropical rainforest with a variety of parrots and rare tropical plants. Admission is less than $10 and it is a great place to escape and read a book.

The Botanical Garden - Don't expect carp-filled ponds and breathtaking flowers. Do expect a serene atmosphere with trails and indigenous foliage. Impress your sweetheart with a picnic lunch here. It is on Stock Island just off College Road.

REASON TO QUIT — #18

I'm tired of winning friends and influencing people.

The Sheriff's Office Animal Farm – Key West may be the only city with a petting zoo operated out of the prison. This keeps a lot of people away, but it is definitely a cool experience. Call the Monroe County Detention Center for the zoo's hours of operation, as they are usually only open Sundays.

A Day at the Bridge – Need to get out of Key West? Take a little trip up to Sugarloaf Key and swing a right at the Sugarloaf Lodge. Park at the end of the street before it turns right and then walk the dirt road back to the bridge over the Government Cut. This is a cool place for snorkeling, sunbathing and swimming. Some people even jump off the bridge though we should let you know that this is illegal. Do it at your own risk and don't tell Mandy we gave her secret spot away.

Nobody Knows – This one you will have to find on your own. It takes some work, but it exists on Stock Island. We like to think of it as the last rough and tough fisherman's bar in town. Once you locate this one you are a true local.

Stupid Questions or Stoopid People?

If you want to fit in as a local you must be aware that you cannot send your brain on a week's vacation at the same time you take yours. Tourist towns are famous for the silly questions people ask and Key West is no different. Here are a few of the gems we have heard in the past and the responses we would have given, had we been asked.

Drag racing! Once a year local drag queens have a sprint down Duval Street.

1. Tourist to bartender: "Do you live in Key West?"
Our Reply: "No, I'm on vacation like you but I thought I'd try to make a few extra dollars."

2. Waiter to tourist: "Our fresh fish of the day is dolphin."
Tourist to waiter: "Oh my god, I can't believe you're serving Flipper!"
Our Reply: "Actually it's Flipper's brother but we do have an authentic Lassie stew that may interest you."

3. Overheard at the post office: "Have you posted tomorrow's mail yet?"
Our reply: "Yes, I'm sorry. That went out yesterday."

4. On Duval Street: "Is Jimmy Buffett playing at Margaritaville tonight?"
Our reply: "Yes, but get there early."

5. To concierge: "It says sunset is at 8:00 p.m. but we have dinner reservations. Is there a later one?"
Our reply: "Due to popular demand the sun now sets every hour on the hour. Be sure to bring sunscreen."

6. Overheard on Christmas Eve: "What time is the midnight mass?"
Our reply: 12 p.m.

7: "Can we snorkel under the island?"
Our reply: "No, I'm sorry. That is reserved exclusively for scuba diving."

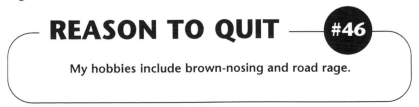

REASON TO QUIT — #46

My hobbies include brown-nosing and road rage.

8: "Do we actually get to meet Ernest when we go to the Hemingway House?"
Our reply: He's on vacation this week, but Shel Silverstein is filling in for him."

9. " How long is the Seven-Mile Bridge?"
Our reply: "About 11.2651 kilometers."

10. "Do you miss the United States?"
Our reply: "Yes, but our King is kind to all his people."

11. "Is it really only 90 miles to Cuba?"
Our reply: "That's right, and on a clear day you can actually see Havana from the Southernmost Point."

12. "How far apart are the mile markers?"
Our answer: "5,280 feet."

13. Overheard on a fishing boat: "What's our current altitude?"
Our answer: "3 feet."

14. "Does the sun always set on this side of the island?"
Our answer: "Only in the winter months. In the summer it sets in the east."

15. "Are all of the bridges manmade?"
Our answer: "Most are, but like Stonehenge, the origin of some is a mystery."

REASON TO QUIT — #85

I own more than one sweater with an animal on it.

Key West Bumper Stickers

Why do they call it tourist season if we can't shoot them?

Key West: Buy one get one free.

Key West: a quaint little drinking town with a tourist problem.

♥NY? Take US1 North!

ONE HUMAN FAMILY

It's our town. Let's keep it clean and green.

If you're not delighted, you're not paying attention.

Slow down! This ain't the mainland.

I'm not a lesbian but my girlfriend is.

What's Up With That?

Answers to questions
you were afraid to ask

You're probably feeling like a pretty cool local right now, despite the fact that you haven't yet told the boss where to stick it. But hold that excitement for one more chapter.

In the next few pages we're going to give you a crash course in local lingo. Some of the terms are unique to Key West, other items will give you a little island background and save you the embarrassment of asking questions that will reveal your newness to the island. As the tourist towns like to say, "There are no stupid questions, just stupid people."

Conchs: The first thing you need to know is the pronunciation. It is Konk, rhymes with honk. You may know it as the mollusk that lives on the ocean floor, but in Key West it also means anybody who was born in Key West. A Freshwater Conch is a resident of at least seven years and an Honorary Conch is anyone the County Mayor sees fit to present the honor to. True Conchs can obtain seniority with each generation and you will find it common to hear people damn proud of the fact that they are a 4th, 5th, or 6th generation Conch. Our phone book has more than 41 businesses listed under Conch.

Bubba: You will hear this term used in two different ways, depending on which side of the system you are on. Some people love to complain about the Bubba System, while others will greet friends, relatives, and acquaintances with "bubba" as a sign of friendship or camaraderie. The term comes from the word brother and started in Key West as a friendly term. In the days when Key West was truly an island, people had to rely on their neighbors and it was a more forgiving town. Police would

Mad Props! Because of noise, certain jet planes are not permitted to fly into Key West.

turn a blind eye, elected officials would help friends, you scratch my back and I'll scratch yours, etc. Favors were common, and the usual response of "Thanks, my Bubba." could be heard all around town. Newcomers to the island who were not fortunate enough to receive this special treatment dubbed the term "Bubba System." The system still exists, so choose your side of the fence wisely.

Rainbow Flags: You will notice rainbows all over Key West. Not rainbows in the sky, but rainbow flags flying in storefronts, rainbow stickers on cars, rainbow T-shirts, rainbow key chains and more. The rainbow is the symbol of the gay community. Rainbow flags or stickers on a storefront indicate the business is gay-owned and operated or gay-friendly, which most are.

The Conch Republic: You will hear this term used interchangeably with Key West, but it only came about in April, 1982 when the federal government put up a roadblock between Miami and the Florida Keys. Traffic jams followed and nobody wanted to come to Key West, so our mayor decided that if we were going to be treated like a foreign country we might as well become one. We seceded from the Union, declared war on the United States, immediately surrendered and asked for a billion dollars in aid. The aid never came through but the point was made and the roadblock came down. The event is celebrated each year during the week of the Conch Republic Independence Celebration.

Mount Trashmore: The closest thing we have to a mountain in Key West is the pile of trash from our old dumping grounds. It boasts the highest elevation in the Keys and probably comes up in everyday

REASON TO QUIT — **#48**

For vacation this year I cleaned the garage.

conversation more often than any dump in the world.

Locals Cards: When you arrive in Key West you will see the stickers on cash registers that promise savings with your Locals Card. The card only costs a few bucks and will save you money, but most businesses will give you the discount even without the card. Get your new driver's license with your Key West address pronto and you can enjoy little perks like avoiding a cover charge, discount parking and 10 to 20% off food and drinks. Don't be afraid to ask places if they give local discounts. Most do.

Beach Closures: We hope this is the first part of the book to become outdated, but if you are going to live here you should know that our water is not the best in the world. In the year 2000 water testing standards changed and it was discovered that our water contains high levels of fecal coliform (that's crap to you and me!) The city spent millions replacing all of our sewer lines, and the beaches are not closed as frequently anymore, but the fecal coliform still exists. Our advice if you can't stay out of the water: go to Fort Zachary Taylor where the currents keep the water clean.

Fantasy Fest: This is the biggest party of the year, also known as the time when all of your friends decide to come visit and don't object to sleeping on the floor. The best way to describe the event is Mardi Gras in Key West. Some people make the mistake of thinking this is a Halloween event, but the fact of the matter is that the big parade is always on the last Saturday of October and the events start the week

Limey Bastards! Spanish Limes taste great but don't get them on your skin or clothes – their stain is nearly impossible to get off.

before with Goombay Festival. Themes change every year as does city policy on nudity and body paint.

Season - Off-Season: We don't have falling leaves or snowflakes, but some people (jackasses) insist that Key West does have seasons. We call them busy season (the time when tourists are here) and off-season (the time when no one is here). Our change in seasons used to be much more dramatic where businesses would literally shut down in the summer months because nobody was here. Though we now have a steady year-round economy people still look forward to season, which starts after Christmas and finishes up in April after spring break. The rest of the year is filled with ups and downs that revolve around different holidays, festivals and events.

Jimmy Buffett: Let's get one thing straight: A buffet is the place where you stuff your face with shrimp egg rolls until your pants split and a Buffett is the guy who sings about Margaritaville. Jimmy Buffett used to live in Key West and still visits occasionally. He still owns a recording studio at the Historic Seaport and still records albums there. Living in Key West for six years we have stalked...er, I mean met, Jimmy Buffett once and have seen him play twice. A favorite local pastime is allowing tourists to overhear a conversation about Jimmy Buffett playing at Margaritaville that night.

Bikes: Don't skip over this section, wise guy. It may sound like an obvious subject but there are a couple of things you should know about owning and riding a bike in Key West. First of all, if you leave your bike unlocked it will be stolen. Secondly, if you leave your bike unlocked it will be stolen. If you ride your bike at night, make sure you

REASON TO QUIT — **#89**

I lie about my profession.

have a bike light. Lanes are narrow, people drive drunk, and not having a light is an invitation for the cops to pull you over. There is a strange phenomenon in Key West where anybody riding their bike at night, without a light, going the wrong way down a one-way street will get pulled over and the police will find drugs on them. Did you know that driving your bicycle while under the influence of alcohol is considered drunk driving and you can lose your license? Go buy a light now, and don't forget to lock your bike either.

Parking: In Key West we traded road rage for parking rage. It is a simple fact that there are more cars in Old Town than there are parking spots. The first thing you need to do is leave your stinking car back where you came from so we can still find a spot for ourselves. Failing that, get your Florida plates that say Monroe County so you can park in the residential parking spots. Frequent visitors to downtown can get monthly parking permits for something upwards of $100. You can always take your chances with parking meters ($1.50 per hour enforced 8 a.m. – 12 a.m. 7 days a week) but you should know that parking meters are a major source of revenue for the city and a $20 ticket will be issued during the three-minute period you ran into the bank. After spending some time in town you will learn about the secret spots and which lots really enforce their towing policy. We could tell you, but then why would we?

Chickens: Why did the chicken cross the road? Because people in Key West needed something else to complain about. For years the chickens

Bar tab? The last liquor license sold in Key West
went for close to $400,000.

and the people of Key West lived in harmony. The chickens provided eggs and meat as well as hours of entertainment in the form of cock-fights and the humans ate the eggs and meat and bet money on the cockfights. Eventually cock-fighting was outlawed and eggs were imported by the dozen. Chicken meat also became available at the store, and though it cost a few dollars more, the price was well worth it to avoid the sight of a headless chicken running around the back yard getting blood everywhere. Suddenly the chicken was not such an important part of island life, and the people who did not rely on them while growing up deemed roosters a nuisance. Near the end of the 20th century, the great chicken controversy began. While some people took great joy in watching young hatchlings following the mama hen across the street, pecking away at the mosquitoes, cockroaches and scorpions, others found no delight in the crowing under their windows at all hours of the night. The controversy continues to this day.

Key Deer: You will hear quite a bit about these little guys, but don't even think about getting your rifle and hunting gear. The Key Deer call Big Pine Key home and are unique because of their size. Descended from your average deer, the Key Deer are much smaller and have the unique ability to drink salt water. They have been on the endangered species list and the population suffers each year as traffic on the high-way increases. The best time to see the deer is at dawn or dusk when they come to the roadside to feed. Pay attention to the strictly posted speed limits as they are strictly enforced.

T-Shirt Shops: Maybe we should have told you about this when you were a tourist and spent $200 for three T-shirts. Be careful where you buy your souvenirs. Many places in town are reasonable and reputable,

REASON TO QUIT — #63

I think the smoke detector is really a video camera.

but there are a number of T-shirt shops that use illegal and deceptive practices to separate you from your money. Some of the scams involve giving you free shirts and then charging exorbitant rates for custom decals, while others involve price switching. The shops are required to provide a written estimate of the cost, but it does not always work out like that. Play it safe and ask for your estimate before any decal is made or the purchase is completed.

Houseboat Row: By the time you read this, Houseboat Row may be gone, but it was the center of controversy for years and is bound to come up in conversation. On the eastern side of the island along South Roosevelt Boulevard was a funky little community of houseboats known as Houseboat Row (creative name, isn't it?). Rent was free until Florida claimed rights to submerged land surrounding the state, which began a legal battle that continued for years. The battle was settled when Hurricane Georges decided to destroy most of the houseboats. As this book goes to print, the city has issued eviction notices to the remaining boats and another chapter of old Key West comes to a close. Miss Cleo predicts a city marina there in the future.
*2007 Update: Houseboat Row is gone, but its legend lives on.

Bone Island: When we get tired of saying Key West or the Conch Republic we can always use Bone Island. When the Spanish discovered Key West in the 16th century the beaches were covered with bones. In the Spanish language Cayo Hueso literally means island of bones. Over the years Cayo was turned into Key and Hueso into West. Talk about boning up on your history.

Merry Christmas? On Christmas Day 1921, Key West had its last tar and feathering.

Dogs: Instead of a leash law, our city ordinances require that your canine be under your control. That's good news for you if Spot will heel when you tell him to. Most people agree that it is pretty cool having all of these dogs roaming around town in the bars and restaurants. Some stores even put water bowls out front to quench their thirst. The downside is that you have to watch your step when you are walking down the street. Attention dog owners: pick up after your dogs or you could be fined $500. Attention cat people: oh, never mind, we know cats don't pay attention.

Dress Codes: Don't worry about being refused service in a restaurant because you are dressed improperly. That won't happen with the exception of the shirt and shoes rule, though often times even that does not apply. The island is hot and humid so shorts will normally do. People here are less judgmental, so whether you are wearing a polo shirt or one that says Iron Maiden you can still dine in some of the finer restaurants. (WARNING: Iron Maiden shirts went out of style in the late 80s.) For the guys reading this who are thinking of bringing down their collection of suits and ties, please be aware that the only time you will wear a suit in Key West is for a wedding, a funeral, and when the judge asks the defendant to please rise.

Movies: Key West has two theaters. One is mainstream with six screens and sticky floors while the other is an art cinema with two screens, beer and wine. Tropic Cinema, just off Duval Street on Eaton, offers independent cinema from across the globe. Classy, entertaining and educational. Did we mention the beer?

REASON TO QUIT — #13

These heels are killing me.

Conch Cruisers: Next time you see that car with the funky paint job, don't smack your friend in the arm and say, "Check out that car with the funky paint job!" In Key West they are known as "Conch Cruisers." Key West can be like a strange car museum. We have had a car shaped like a chili pepper, one painted with maple leaves, a Duster with a giant egg on top that reads "Eat Me," cars covered with tile, with plants, with beads…Some bikes are also called "Conch Cruisers." They have one gear and back pedal brakes.

Stock Island: Stock Island is the closest island to Key West. It was originally called Live-stock Island because that was where they kept most of the animals. The place will probably be a real estate goldmine when they run out of space to build in Key West, but currently it is a bit more affordable than the main island. Most of the homes on Stock Island are trailers, making it the butt of redneck jokes.

Drag Queens: Boys will be _____. Did you say girls? Score two points. Key West has a group of guys who dress up as girls on a regular basis. Most cities have drag queens, but in Key West your chances of running into them are much better. With names like Mama Crass, Sushi, Inga, and Scabola Feces, your life in Key West is not complete until you have seen one of the drag shows these ladies put on. The best spot for a drag queen sighting is the 800 block of Duval Street.

Mini Lobster Season: Florida lobster is nothing like the Maine lobster that has become such a delicacy. Unfortunately, restaurants still charge

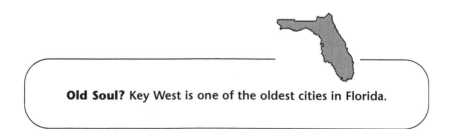

Old Soul? Key West is one of the oldest cities in Florida.

a good price because it is lobster. The main difference (no pun intended, but you can laugh anyway) is that Florida, or Caribbean, lobsters don't have large claws like their brothers from the North. Imagine a giant crayfish. Cold water seafood tends to be better than warm water seafood, so Florida lobster is a bit chewier as well. Despite all of this, people like to eat them and your average Joe is given two days every year to jump in the water with a lobster assassination kit before commercial fishermen hit the water. This usually falls around the end of July and lobsters are limited to six per person per day. The lobster must have a three-inch carapace. Regular lobster season runs August 6 through March 31.

VICES

You really don't need to know any of the information that follows. Like us, you are a model citizen, a pillar of society; some may even say a saint. Too bad all of your friends can't be so good. Go ahead and read this section so you can give your pals good information. In this section we'll give you the skinny on sex, drugs and alcohol.

Drinking: The legal drinking age in Key West is 21. If you are not 21, you should be aware that the Department of Alcohol, Tobacco and Firearms likes to go undercover to various bars and they won't mind arresting you. Alcohol can be served legally at bars until 4:00 a.m. but it is not available on Sunday until after noon. Key West has an open container law, which means you cannot walk the streets with an alcoholic beverage. The police will often turn a blind eye if your drink is in a plastic cup, but know that if you are causing problems they can still arrest you for an open container. Grocery stores sell beer and wine and

REASON TO QUIT — **#77**

Fifteen minutes just isn't enough time for coffee and a cigarette.

liquor stores, well, they sell liquor. Before you decide to drink and drive in Key West you should consider that a taxi ride anywhere on the island does not exceed $15 and if you drive drunk you will probably know the person you kill.

After-hours: Some people just can't get enough. Often, when the bars close in the wee hours of the morning, someone will invite everybody back to their house for more drinking and debauchery. These are known as after-hours parties. They are good if you are a friend, bad if you are a neighbor.

Strip Clubs: Good news, guys: Key West usually has four or five strip bars in operation at any given time. Unlike most of the United States, the girls in these clubs get totally naked. Expect the girls to ask if you would like a lap dance. They cost $20 plus tip per song and involve the girl getting naked and grinding around on your lap. It's a small town, so tip the girls on stage at least a dollar per song. Sorry, ladies, there is only one club with male strippers and they usually dance for other men.

Nude Beaches: Key West does not have any. If you are looking for the sun to shine where the sun don't shine, head to the Garden of Eden located high above Duval Street in the same building as the Bull and Whistle bars.

Sex Shops: Key West has a number of shops where you can purchase everything from dirty magazines to blow-up sheep. Some are open 24 hours a day and Leathermaster will custom design a variety of toys for you. If you're just looking for some dirty magazines try Truman Avenue Books.

Ouch! There is no hospital in Key West.
The closest one is one island away.

Prostitution: Our lawyers want us to tell you that prostitution is illegal and you could catch diseases and die. We want to tell you that it's pretty sad if you have to pay someone for sex. Prostitution is not as common in Key West as you might expect. Forget the strip clubs because that is not what they are about. You may find a crack whore on the side streets that will do the deed with you, but let's get real. We do have a couple of places that are similar to massage parlors where you pay a flat fee to get in and then negotiate the price for services directly with the girl (or guy) but be prepared to spend some serious cash. Our Yellow Pages list four escort services. Enjoy.

Drugs: As we said earlier, everyone who comes to Key West is escaping something. It can also be said that people take drugs to escape. Put the two together and you have a lot of drugs in Key West. Let's break them down into categories.

<u>Pot</u>: We've never known so many people who smoke pot. Doctors, lawyers, politicians, old people, young people, fat people, skinny people, rich people, poor people; everyone smokes pot. Hardly a day goes by that we don't smell pot wafting down an Old Town lane. Though there is a lot of pot on the island it can be difficult to find. It all goes back to the small island theory. We have 25,000 people living here and it's easy to get caught in a small town. No drug dealer in his right mind is going to sell pot to a stranger. Our advice: get to know people who smoke, which is pretty much anyone, and take it from there.

<u>Cocaine</u>: What do you think the chances are of finding cocaine on an island where people work three jobs? If you said "good," score two points. There is a lot of coke on the island, but don't look to us to hook

REASON TO QUIT — **#65**

I can't really think of a reason not to quit.

you up. It's amazing how many tourists ask bartenders where they can get drugs. Do they really think the bartender is going to risk their job and prison for a guy who tips them two bucks on a five-dollar drink? If you are looking for cocaine, hang around people who are doing it. If you've done it before you will know who they are. If you have not done it before, don't start now. Don't listen to anyone who tells you to buy drugs in Bahama Village. You might get a crack rock, but your chances are better of being ripped off or arrested in one of the many reverse stings.

Ecstasy: Word on the street says you can still find it with a little searching, but ecstasy is not as plentiful as it was during the millennium.

Other drugs: Choose your poison and someone here can probably get it for you. When dealing with drugs (no pun intended) follow these rules.

1. Drugs are illegal. If you get arrested, everyone will know.
2. Don't buy drugs from strangers.
3. If you go out in public on drugs, you will see people you know, possibly your boss.
4. "I took three pills last night" is not a valid excuse for calling in sick to work.

Beaches? We don't need no stinking beaches! Higgs Beach is actually an African burial ground. Smathers Beach was once home to a slaughterhouse and cow teeth can still be found there.

In Closing
Words of Wisdom

Quitting a job is something everyone should do at least once. Jobs provide some great necessities such as money and insurance and they can also provide stability, morale and the feeling of accomplishment that lets us go to sleep at night knowing we have made a difference. These are good things that benefit us all, but unfortunately with the good can come the bad.

How many of us have been the victim of a vicious rumor in the workplace or taken the blame for something that was not our fault? How many of us have pitched in and gone the extra mile without receiving so much as a thank you when the work was done? How many of us have fallen prey to politics in the workplace and been helpless to defend ourselves?

Work has undergone significant change in the last 20 years and shows no sign of stopping. Computerization and other factors have created a cookie-cutter work environment where creativity is discouraged rather than encouraged and companies still have a way of making us feel as though we would be lost without them. Do you recall the last person who left your workplace on his or her own terms? Everyone probably wished them well and then talked about whether they would survive out there, before the door was even closed. Do you remember the last time you left a job on your own terms? It felt pretty good, didn't it?

Humans tend to think the grass is always greener on the other side of the fence when in reality the grass is just a different shade of green and probably tastes a little different too. A wise man once said that variety is the spice of life, but the bottom line is this: No matter where you work or where you live, life will be what you make of it.

Some of you probably got this book as a neat little gift from a

REASON TO QUIT — #33

I've always wanted to be a pirate.

friend who visited Key West; some of you were probably surprised with it by your husband or wife after your vacation was over. Either way, we hope you learned a lot about Key West. We worked hard gathering information that was exciting and helpful as well as demonstrative of some differences in everyday life that are experienced in Key West. Some of the information you probably knew already and heaven knows you don't need us to tell you the proper way to quit a job, but that is not the point.

Everybody has dreams but not everyone follows them. If we had a dollar for every visitor to the island who said they wanted to quit their job and move to Key West we would be very wealthy men. It is a popular dream and an obtainable one. (Moving here, not us getting a dollar for everyone who does.) If this book took your mind off the pressures of everyday life for a while and let you fantasize about living in paradise, we have done our job. From here on out you are on your own. We quit!

Grave situation! The actual island is made of coral and limestone, which makes it difficult to dig more than a couple of inches. For this reason, most of our burials are above ground.

RobOneal.com

About The Author

David L. Sloan went insane in 1996 and a little voice in his head told him to quit the corporate world and move to Key West. It was later discovered that the voice was one of his multiple personalities. He is the founder of Sloan's Ghost Hunt and author of numerous books.

While David is frequently called "the next Hemingway" this reference is usually applied to his penchant to drinking and death – rarely to his writing. David lives in Key West with his cat, Dr. Jeckyll. Upon completion of this book he plans to pursue his career as a rock star.

David's Job Timeline
What a long strange trip it's been!

1. Age 11: Lawn Mower ....Quit
2. Age 16: Counter Boy at Purdy's ....Quit
3. Age 17: Baker ....Quit
4. Age 18: Little Caesar's Pizza ...Quit before being fired
5. Age 19: Chef's Apprentice ....Quit
6. Age 20: Housekeeping Supervisor ....Promoted
7. Age 21: Front Desk Supervisor ....Quit
8. Age 22: Hotel Night Manager ....Quit
9. Age 23: Cruise Ship General Manager ....Quit
10. Age 26: Husband ....Fired
11. Age 26: Ghost Tour Owner ....Still there in spirit
12. Age 28: Writer/Publisher ....Still There
13. Age 31: Famous Author ....Not Quite

Special Thanks

Thank you Chris Shultz for your friendship, ideas, work ethics and wicked sense of humor. Kerry Karshna for incredible set-up and design. Mandy Bolen for master editing. Mattey Casey, Elizabeth Johnson and Larry Stanford for editing and creative input. Rob O'Neal for photos. Thank you Joan Langley and Langley Press for always being there. Michael Keith, June Keith and Palm Island Press for making things happen.

This book would not have been possible without the support of my family and friends – you know who you are.

Musical inspiration provided by Ween.

RobOneal.com

About The Author

Christopher Shultz grew up in Minnesota and went to Emerson College in Boston where he earned a B.S. in Visual and Media Arts. He came to Key West from Los Angeles to pursue a film opportunity, but was soon sucked into the magic of the Key West bars. One day he woke to find himself a bartender. Christopher has quit several jobs and even been fired from a couple (including the one he woke up in.) After finishing this book he plans to pursue his dream of becoming a filmmaker by producing his first feature film LUCID. If that doesn't work out he plans to become a superhero and failing that, he wants to sing Tom Waits songs for spare change in New York subways.

Christopher's Job Timeline

Here is a list of the jobs I have had in the past. Some were fun and some were not but they were all okay to say goodbye to.

1.	Age 14:	Bagboy	Quit
2.	Age 15:	Bingo Guy	Quit
3.	Age 16:	Software assembler	Quit
4.	Age 18:	Busboy	Quit
5.	Age 18:	Telemarketer	Quit
6.	Age 18:	Production assistant	Job Ended
7.	Age 18:	Software assembler	Quit
8.	Age 19:	Waiter	Quit
9.	Age 19:	Club Promoter	Quit
10.	Age 21:	Bartender	Quit
11.	Age 22:	Dog walker	Quit
12.	Age 22:	Tech support	Quit
13.	Age 22:	Script reader	Quit
14.	Age 23:	Video Production/Web Design	Quit
15.	Age 24:	Bartender	Fired
16.	Age 25:	Bartender	Fired
17.	Age 26:	Filmmaker/Author	Self Employed

Special Thanks

Thank you to everyone who helped make this book possible and stood by all of my warped ideas.

My friends and family: Patricia and Jeffery Palmer for their love, Mary Ellen Harrison for her inspiration, Susy Adlis, Jevne, Ben Anderson, Silke and Keith St. Peter, Jorge, Ann & Mike Marrero for their friendship and David Sloan, one of the strangest people I've ever met.

Chris Shultz

Extra special thanks to Lisa Corey for her never ending understanding patience and love.

(Told ya I'd get a picture of you in here.)

111

About The Photographer

When choosing someone to shoot pictures for this book, we did not have to look far. Not only is Rob O'Neal an excellent photographer, he is also a friend.

In 1996 after sixteen years of serving up grub for obnoxious diners, Rob quit his job as a waiter and came to Key West to pursue his love of photography.

He has shot rock stars, Presidents and more sunset weddings than he cares to admit. His work can be seen daily in the Key West Citizen as well as online at **RobOneal.com**.

Check out some of Rob's Cuba photographs at **cubashots.com**.

Rob resides in Key West with his dog Jagger.

"*And if it doesn't work out there'll never be any doubt that the pleasure was worth all the pain.*"

– Jimmy Buffett

Supermodels

Truman archival: Harry Truman

Southernmost Point: This photo features British super-model Justin Bowden, who graciously risked public nudity charges while changing costumes behind the buoy. Thank you, Justin.

End of the rainbow: Rob O'Neal, Patricia Palmer, Silke St. Peter, Lauren Hulnick, Kerry Karshna, Elizabeth Johnson, Mattey Casey, Chris Shultz, David Sloan

Will work for booze: Larry Stanford

Beach babes: Sandra Guthrie, Charlene Brown

Test takers: Gregg McGrady, Sid Jordan

Winter cold: Charlene Brown, Gregory Hummel

Conch train: Stephanie Nelson, Al Nelson

Wild thing: Mattey Casey

What's up: Adrian Baker

Thanks to all of our supermodels.

For additional copies of this book

1. Send a check or money order for $14.95 to:
   Phantom Press – Quit
   1311 Catherine Street
   Key West, FL 33040

2. Visit our web site: http://www.amazon.com

3. Go to the bookstore where you got this copy.

Editor's Note:

These pages were not intentionally left blank. The authors quit before editing was completed, leaving the rest up to you. If you see David and Chris, tell them the printer wants his money.

Also Available From Phantom Press:

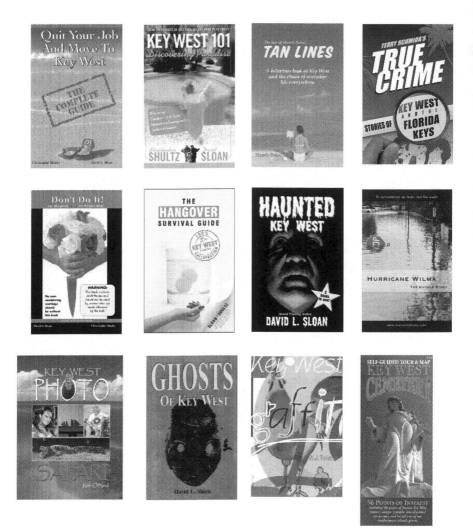

Well, what are you waiting for? Quit already!

Made in the USA
Charleston, SC
14 November 2016